CONSUMING PASSIONS

By the same author

DECODING ADVERTISEMENTS:
Ideology and Meaning in Advertising

Judith Williamson
CONSUMING PASSIONS

The Dynamics
of Popular Culture

MARION BOYARS

LONDON   NEW YORK

Published in Great Britain and the United States
in 1986 by Marion Boyars Publishers
24 Lacy Road, London, SW15 1NL and
262 West 22nd Street, New York, NY 10011

Distributed in the United States by
The Scribner Book Companies Inc

Distributed in Canada by
Collier Macmillan Canada Inc

Distributed in Australia by
Wild and Woolley, Glebe, N.S.W.

British Library Cataloguing in Publication Data
Williamson, Judith, 1954–
    Consuming passions: the dynamics of popular culture.
    1. Great Britain — Social conditions — 1945–
    I. Title
    941.085'8   HN385.5

Library of Congress Cataloging in Publication Data
Williamson, Judith, 1954–
    Consuming passions.
    Bibliography: p.
    1. Popular culture — History — 20th century.
    2. Great Britain — Popular culture — History — 20th century.
    3. United States — Popular culture — History — 20th century.
    4. Consumers. I. Title.
    CB430.W55   1985   306'.4   85–11194

ISBN 0–7145–2828–5 Cloth
ISBN 0–7145–2851–X Pbk

Photoset by Fleetlines Ltd., Southend-on-Sea.

Printed and bound in Great Britain by
Robert Hartnoll (1985) Ltd., Bodmin, Cornwall

To the memory
of my father
Tom Williamson
1915–1985

CONTENTS

FOREWORD

With the exception of half a dozen new pieces, the articles and essays in this book have been written over a period of about eight years, and first appeared in a variety of publications. I have not made any fundamental alterations to them since retrospective editing would, in a sense, turn them all into products of the present. However, where significant alterations were made by these publications I have reinstated my own versions, and included sections that were cut through lack of space. Where my original title for a piece differs from the one it was published under, I have used the original but indicated the published title at the end.

These minor changes aside, I have let the work stand; for despite the stretch of time over which they were written, the articles share certain concerns and perspectives and, I believe, add up to an investigation of some of the many forms in which passions are consumed.

I am grateful to all the publications which have commissioned and printed my work, but I would particularly like to mention City Limits magazine, having been a founder member of the co-operative, and I would like to thank all its workers, past and present. I also want to thank Helen Dady, who typed the final manuscript, Katherine Shonfield and Janet Williamson, for their perceptive comments on many pieces, Don MacPherson, who co-wrote 'Prisoner of Love' and whose generous encouragement helped me get the whole project off the ground, and Brand Thumim, whose advice and support have been invaluable to me during the completion of this book.

INTRODUCTION: 'CONSUMING PASSIONS'

We are consuming passions all the time – at the shops, at the movies, in the streets, in the classroom: in the old familiar ways that no longer seem passionate because they are the shared paths of our social world, the known shapes of our waking dreams. Passions born out of imbalance, insecurity, the longing for something *more,* find forms in the objects and relations available; so that energies fired by what might be, become the fuel for maintaining what already is. Every desire that needs to be dulled, every sharpness at the edge of consciousness that needs to be softened, every yearning that tries to tear through some well-worn weakness in the fabric of daily life, must be woven back into that surface to strengthen it against such exposure. 'Consuming passions' can mean many things: an all-embracing passion, a passion for consumerism; what I am concerned with is the way passions are themselves consumed, contained and channelled into the very social structures they might otherwise threaten.

The subject most avidly consumed in academic work over recent years has been 'desire', which has gained prestige in the theoretical world as a 'radical' topic. But in our society where sensuality is frozen, arrested in the streets of our cities, stretched out over every surface, public imagery has accustomed us to a sexuality that is served up in slices, and theory offers the cold slab of the dissecting table to further this operation. For academic interest in 'desire' is not unrelated to the obsession with 'revealing' sex on every hoarding. People who study things aren't fuelled by different drives from anyone else. Desire has become the subject of numerous books, conferences, articles, lunchtime lectures and so on; but the drive to read endless articles about it in theoretical journals has ultimately the same impetus as the drive to read endless articles about it in *Cosmopolitan* or *Over 21;* it is just that academic work satisfies both appetite *and* duty, and gives an important sense of control. Desire itself is channelled into this endless, obsessive theorizing about desire – harnessed in its own pursuit; and with theory, as with sex, the more elusive its object, the more interesting this pursuit is.

But passion – passion is another story. It is to be written *about,* but not *with:* for the essence of all this academic work on 'desire' is to *stay cool.* In the dominant ideology of our culture, and particularly its more 'intellectual' layers, it has never been fashionable to *over-invest* in any activity. And the bourgeois etiquette whereby any violent display of feeling is automatically taboo, any raising of the voice rude no matter what the reason, merely sets out the pattern of a much wider social phenomenon, the consensus by which any form of the 'extreme' is outlawed. Passions are fine on the cinema screen or in hi-fi advertisements – but not on the demonstration or picket line. For in the peculiar but familiar customs of consumer capitalism, our emotions are directed towards objects, rather than actions.

Marx talks of the commodity as 'congealed labour', the frozen form of a past activity; to the consumer it is also congealed longing, the final form of an active wish. And the shape in which fulfilment is offered seems to become the shape of the wish itself. The need for change, the sense that there must be something else, something different from the way things are, becomes the need for a new purchase, a new hairstyle, a new coat of paint. Consuming products does give a thrill, a sense of both belonging and being different, charging normality with the excitement of the unusual; like the Christmas trips of childhood to Oxford Street, to see the lights – and the lighted windows, passions leaping through plate-glass, filling the forms of a hundred products, tracing the shapes of a hundred hopes. The power of purchase – taking home a new thing, the anticipation of unwrapping – seems to drink up the desire for something new, the restlessness and unease that must be engendered in a society where so many have so little active power, other than to withdraw the labour which produces its prizes. These objects which become the aims of our passions are also shored up to protect us from them, the bricks of a dam held together by the very force it restrains. Passion is a longing that breaks beyond the present, a drive to the future, and yet it must be satisfied in the forms of the past.

For passion has no form of its own and yet, like the wind, is only revealed in forms; not a ready-made object, it is what breathes life into objects, transforming movement into shape. It is not found in things, but in ways of doing things; and the *ways* things are done are another kind of shape, less solid to our touch than products, but equally forms in which passions are consumed. These forms, not merely of objects but of our activities, provide at once our passions' boundaries and their expression: they are a shared language, for the shapes of our consciousness run right through society, we inhabit the same spaces, use the same things, speak in the same words. The same structures are found at every 'level': the property laws that underpin bourgeois capital also govern personal relationships, marriage, sex, parenthood; the deferred gratification of emotional investment mirrors the very forms and strategies of economic investment. And they are found on every 'side': the back-to-nature organic commune in Wales or California reveals many of the qualities and values of capitalist 'private enterprise' and distaste for urban politics; the need for constant change in 'radical' styles reflects a consumer system based on built-in obsolescence. The forms of oppression frequently provide the mould for its resistance; thus the Labour Party sets itself the task of producing a strong 'leader' to 'match' Mrs Thatcher, rather than questioning the *terms* of 'leadership' in the air at the last election. And the highly visible, individual violence focused on by the media in mining communities during the miners' strike, exists in exact proportion to the less immediately visible, social violence of the plans that have caused it – plans for closures which could ravage those communities in an ultimately much more far-reaching way.

The dominant political notion in Britain has been for decades that of a 'consensus': there are agreed limits to what is and is not acceptable, and although these are constantly shifting, they must always be seen as fixed, since they form the ground-plan of social stability. The shapes of an era are more easily found in its fashions, its furniture, its buildings – whose lines do seem to trace the 'moods' of social change – than in the equally significant outlines of its thoughts and habits, its conceptual categories, which are harder to see because they are precisely what we take for granted.

How then *can* we 'see' them? If it is in shapes and forms that passions live – as lightning lives in a conductor – it is likely to be in images – in films, photographs, television – that such conduits are most clearly visible. Our emotions are wound into these forms, only to spring back at us with an apparent life of their own. Movies seem to *contain* feelings, two-dimensional photographs seem to *contain* truths. The world itself seems filled with obviousness, full of natural meanings which these media merely reflect. But *we* invest the world with its significance. It doesn't have to be the way it is, or to mean what it does. Who doesn't know, privately, that sense that desire lives, not in ourselves, but in the form of the person desired – in the features of their face, the very lines of their limbs? The contours of our social world are equally charged, the shapes of public life equally evocative, of passions that are in fact our own. And in the most crucial areas of meaning, public and private intersect: for example, in the way that 'Woman' carries a weight of meanings and passions hived off from the social and political world and diverted into 'sexuality', a process seen at its crudest in the way Britain's highest circulation daily paper replaces news with the page 3 pin-up. The whole drive of our society is to translate social into individual forms: movements are represented by 'leaders' ('Arthur Scargill's strike'), economic problems are pictured as personal problems ('too lazy to get a job'), public values are held to be private values ('let the family take over from the Welfare State').

This transformation of social forces into individual terms is not inevitable; but we are used to the same old furnishings of our conceptual world and frightened to grope around in the dark for different ones. It is a relief when half-formed fantasies, new outlines struggling out of old arrangements, fall back into their familiar shapes, daylight certainties stripped of danger. But even in the yearning for normality, for conformity, can be found the passion for a shared world; a sense of possibility expressed in the sensation of the obvious. There is a kind of poignancy for the way things *are*, when the familiar seems to contain more than itself: in the way that a landscape can be filled with longing, a street – as in so many songs – paved with passions. *('I get a funny feeling inside of me, just walking up and down – Maybe it's because I'm a Londoner that I love London Town'.)* There is a passion when you glimpse what could be in what already is – in a lighted bus through a winter city, on a summer's day in a public park. In the present forms of our passions it is possible to trace, not only how they are consumed, but the very different future they might ultimately produce.

MODERN GIRL

He wakes and says hello
Turns on the breakfast show
She fixes coffee while he takes a shower
Hey that was great he said
I wish we could stay in bed
But I've got to be at work in less than an hour
She manages a smile as he walks out the door
She's a Modern Girl who's been through this movie before
She don't build her world round no single man
But she's getting by doing what she can
She is free to be
What she wants to be
What she wants to be
Is a Modern Girl
Na na na na na
Na na na na na
Na na na na na
She's a Modern Girl

It looks like rain again
She takes the train again
She's on her way again through London town
She eats a tangerine

Flicks through a magazine
Until it's time to leave her dreams on the underground
She walks to the office like everyone else
An independent lady taking care of herself
She don't build her world round no single man
But she's getting by doing what she can
She is free to be
What she wants to be
What she wants to be
Is a Modern Girl
Na na na na na
Na na na na na
Na na na na na
She's a Modern Girl

She's been dreaming 'bout him all day long . . .
Soon as she gets home
It's him on the telephone
He asks her to dinner, She says I'm not free
Tonight I'm going to stay at home and watch my TV
I don't build my world round no single man
But I'm getting by doing what I can
I am free to be
What I want to be
What I want to be
Is a Modern Girl
Na na na na na
Na na na na na
Na na na na na
She's a Modern Girl

Bugatti/Musker, '*Modern Girl*'
(for Sheena Easton)

WHEN WOMEN WERE WOMEN
AND MEN WERE MEN

'For girls who *don't* want to wear the trousers' runs the copy
of a London underground ad for tights. Now strangely
enough, when I was first allowed out of socks in the
mid-sixties, tights were Freedom Fighters for Liberation,
and featured prominently in images of women hopping in
and out of aeroplanes, wielding guns, and otherwise
engaged in demanding, up-to-the-minute activities. So how
come panti-hose has become the prerogative of girls in
flimsy dresses who look as if they couldn't, but more
importantly, *wouldn't* do anything remotely less feminine
than be bought a Babycham? And how come it is now seen
as a defiant *'choice'* to be feminine?

If being female was the same thing as being feminine the
question wouldn't arise. But femininity, like any representation, needs to be defined *against* something else; and as that
something else shifts, so does our image of 'femininity'. For
example, another recent underground ad shows a woman's
white-stockinged legs standing out amongst a train seat of
pin-striped male legs. Femininity is clearly marked in
contrast to the masculinity of businessmen. But there's
something new here: it's also marked in contrast to the
'masculinity' of being a business*woman:* for the image, in
which everyone, including the woman, has an executive

briefcase and 'top' newspaper, is also about professional equality. And the notion of this equality is a precondition for the ad's way of showing sexual difference – it has to 'kick off' against something, the 'unfemininity' of the professional woman's job.

'Girls who don't want to wear the trousers' seems to be disarmingly simple in its appeal as though it meant 'girls who don't want to be men'. Of course what it really means is 'girls who don't want to be feminists': the contrast isn't with men, but with other, 'liberated' women. For the women's movement has made possible a new form of definition for femininity: one that kicks off *against feminism*.

I am deliberately introducing Jeannette Kupfermann's book, *The MsTaken Body,* in this context because it is so very much for girls who don't want to wear the trousers, and so very dependent (even for publication) on precisely what she attacks – the efforts of people she refers to as 'The Libbers'. Despite setting itself up as a cosmic opposition to the women's movement, this book could only, historically, have come after it. It is also a symptom of something very real, best illustrated by a recent Guardian Women's fashion page which without a hint of irony described the need for frills and flounces in times of economic hardship and distress. Obviously any book is part of a historical climate of feeling but it needs special emphasis here because Kupfermann herself leaps from century to century and from Africa to New Guinea, in describing Woman and Her Symbols – while I for my part read her book with an interest in women and our symbols here and now.

The main thesis of *The MsTaken Body* is that 'symbolism can protect the body' and that the kinds of symbols and rituals found in societies where women have well-defined roles, and where women's and men's activities are clearly demarcated, afford women greater protection and happiness than in our society. But this summary makes Kupfermann's argument sound less confused than it actually is, because despite her anti-modern-rationality-technology stance she never seems to say what she really *feels*. Instead she quotes and cites a hodge-podge of writers and anthropologists, on the following lines;

'Modern physics reveals that all life is based on a system of opposites and their dynamic interplay and exchange . . . to deny male and female is to preclude any possibility of interchange and to promote a breakdown of exchange at the level of the body itself . . . the increasing problems women experience with their bodies relate to the blurring of the lines between the sexes, the trend towards bisexuality, the loss of opposites' . . . men's presence at childbirth is indicative of male 'identity crisis' . . . women in rigid Hassidic societies suffer no 'problems of meaning' . . . there is 'no such thing as rape' in the Arapesh people of New Guinea, where women are excluded from ceremonies and perform clearly separate tasks from the men . . . in religious or community groups, 'mental health is as much facilitated by the social structure, i.e. the rigid separation of men and women and their roles, and the accompanying ritual, as by the ideological imperatives . . .' and so on and so on.

While her point about women's segregation being a form of protection is fairly clear, what is *not* clear is what she suggests we do about it, since all her examples are from small, non-industrial, tribal societies, which could only correspond to this country in pre-capitalist times. The strongest note in all this is really one of nostalgia, not for a remembered, but an imagined past: a world where Women were Women and Men were Men, where a profusion of symbols and rituals spun a soft cocoon around women, wrapped us in a safe space, cushioned us from the world, from men, from pressures and decisions and violence and our own sexual demands and from writing books and dealing with publishers and filling in tax forms and writing articles for deadlines . . . I could go on for ever, which of us couldn't? How often, crippled with period pains, I have wished someone would stand up and offer me a seat in the underground. Locked in a heavy industrial dispute, I want to look pretty, because I'm trying to be tough. How I wish there was some way of being a woman in the 1980s without endlessly battling and struggling to be as good as men while feeling threatened as a woman, uncertain of roles at work and at home, wanting security *and* trying to get taken seriously etc. etc. This is obviously very much what Jeannette Kupfermann feels too – but I wish she'd come right out and *say* it.

More important, this uncertainty and confusion and fear of being undermined are also felt by millions of other women; and the reason this book is so pernicious is that it actually *blames the women's movement* for our problems – even, would you believe it, for period pains. 'The dismal inventory of some of the leading feminists' battles with their own bodies – the depressions, the abortions, the dysmenorrhoea, the painful labours, the weight problems, menopausal horrors – provide a sad statement of cosmic disconnection; they have lost, abandoned, thrown away their symbols, and the price they pay is their own body.'

Most of such surface arguments in *The MsTaken Body* aren't worth refuting in detail, since I expect most readers of this article would disagree with them anyway. The idea of feminists 'paying the price' of dysmenorrhoea and suchlike is ridiculous, a punishment for being naughty girls. What really matters is *why* Ms. Kupfermann is so angry with 'them' (us); what is this sense of loss which is so profound and which is laid at the door of 'the feminists'?

The problem, according to Ms. Kupfermann, is 'symbol starvation'. Because of 'The Libbers', 'women are being educated [does she think all women are passive?] only to understand the literal, physical meaning of their bodies, and to know nothing of their symbolic values.' Or again, 'An attempt has been made to destroy the symbol of women's bodies, and we have been left with a physical husk.' 'The symbolic aspects of the body have been largely ignored or denied by the women's movement – hardly surprising for the symbolic generally is disparaged and underestimated by all Marxist-inspired movements.'

Apart from all the errors – Marxist movements have *not* all disparaged the symbolic, and feminism is *not* a Marxist-inspired movement – there are two extraordinary assumptions here. The first is that women's bodies just 'have' symbolic values – those values that feminists have 'thrown away' (we should be so lucky!) or taught women 'to know nothing of', the symbol that 'an attempt has been made to destroy'. It's as though our bodies had cosmic and eternal meanings that we have chosen, temporarily, to ignore, but in the right frame of mind we might win back again. This isn't a parody, for Kupfermann quotes Jung and his ideas of 'the male and female modes of our psyche', as though these modes were quite separate from social life and imagery.

The second extraordinary assumption shows plain blind ignorance of all the current debates and work within the women's movement and feminist writing. This is the assumption that feminists plan to 'get rid of symbols'. It takes only the most elementary understanding of social communications to realize that you couldn't 'throw away' symbols even if you wanted to, and the whole direction of recent feminist thought has been increasingly to intervene and try to *change* symbols, to engage in struggle *within* the symbolic, and precisely to understand how our bodies and our images are used as part of a network of social meanings. Women are also searching for new symbols of ourselves, our bodies – for symbols that mean something to *us*.

For the enormous aspect of meaning that Kupfermann leaves out, is *who* the symbols she is so keen on have meaning *for*. When Kupfermann says women have always been symbolic, she surely means that women have had meaning *for men*. We have had to interpret our own 'meaning' through their eyes. The 'primitive' societies which she cites as examples of harmony and happiness, and our own society with its films and bill-boards and TV, are alike in that women's main symbolic value is to men – we *are* the language that is spoken on posters and screens, inasmuch as 'Woman' is an image.

The suggestion *The MsTaken Body* makes is that we claim that language as our own, and that we will be happier and have less body-problems if we do. Kupfermann says of glamour and beauty culture that 'through communications it unites women in a way no other comparable culture can or does'. She even asserts that women in psychiatric institutions can be 'cured' by it: 'One tested way of helping to bring them back is via the beauty culture. A new hairdo and lipstick has been known to do more for these women than a month's chemotherapy, for by helping them to use symbols again – to *regain* myths – they are being helped back into the world.'

But whose world? Why is it that women whose roles *are* more clearly defined and separate from men's, e.g. housewives with young children, suffer from worse psychological distress than any other group? Aren't they using enough lipstick? The one thing missing from this whole book is any mention of real social conditions and the structure of power we live under. The kind of protection which Kupfermann refers to time and again is connected with suppression and with inferiority – with treating women like children, and excluding us from public life. And if women really occupied the kinds of roles she suggests, she certainly wouldn't get her book published and mass-produced for £1.95; she'd be completely fulfilled breastfeeding babies and looking glamorously symbolic. Because, when it comes down to it, anyone writing a book doesn't want just to *be* symbolic. I sense something patronizing in that Kupfermann seems to advocate Myth as a panacea for Other Women, while *writing about myth* as a career for herself – just like Nietzsche.

There is this woman.
Watch her.

She is a tapestry
of delicious contradictions.
Capable of laughter
that all the world may witness.
And of tears that
no one will ever see.
A swimmer who may never
enter the water.
A musician who may choose
to listen rather than to play.
A wife who feels like a lover.
A mother who remembers
what it was like to be a child.
There is this woman.
And here is the fragrance
that defines her.
We call it – Cabriole.

Cabriole
by Elizabeth Arden
Because never before has there
been a better, more rewarding time
to be a woman.

23

М.З. с переводчиком
ил. критиком (Марина Юдкевич)

And the social implication of what she suggests is total stasis: not just reactionary, but also impossible, thank goodness.

All the same, underlying her invective is a very real feeling which can't be dismissed without dishonesty. There is a valid reaction against some of the more 'puritanical' aspects of feminism, there is a deep-felt unease about social roles at a time of economic decline and rapid change: there is a recognition that women *have* formed ways of supporting, and communicating with, each other through traditional and 'non-feminist' channels – but the funny thing is, few feminists would dispute all this. Nor would many people dispute that lack of rituals of some sorts – mourning, for example – makes profound change or loss harder to deal with today, when we have few 'rites of passage'. There are points like this which I agree with in her strange book; but it is her anger which is so revealing, and so misplaced, directed as it is against the women's movement rather than the late capitalist society in which our personal and social crises are taking place.

Kupfermann ends her book with the claim that 'the Eternal Feminine was the eternal outsider, and I for one, would never wish to relinquish that position.' But that position, of 'eternal outsider', is precisely one embedded *in* society: that internal space for the 'other' which gives the sense of wholeness Kupfermann quotes so often. She *doesn't* want to be outside, she wants to be snugly wrapped up *inside,* in a space marked 'Eternal Feminine'. This safe enclosure of 'mysticism, irrationality, gentleness, and Beauty' (as she describes it) can be held up to compensate or justify the total lack of these qualities in any other part of society. How long can women go on bearing the values that society wants off its back? When are we going to kick those values into the office, the factory, the housing estate? Kupfermann's fear of 'losing' her symbolic values can surely only be equal to the fear of those in power of having to *act* on those values, and to incorporate them into the social and symbolic life of women *and* men, no matter *who* wears the trousers.

(The Leveller, 1981)

THE LEG-WARMER SYNDROME

The publicity for Pan's new 'Pavanne' romance series relies heavily on the Leg-Warmer Syndrome. This trend was apparent with the tall, sleek women in leotards and leg-warmers who, in a moment of respite from dancing practise, revealed that they did *something* every year, *something else* every month, and took the *Daily Mail* every day. The pages of *Cosmopolitan* and *Honey* are full of these modern creatures, whose independence appears in direct proportion to the quantity and brightness of the gear they keep fit in. Throw in a leg-warmer, the advertising departments must say, and there you have the New Woman.

This seems to have been the case down at 'Pavanne'. *Cosmo, Good Housekeeping, Over 21,* and *Options* are to be saturated with such images in the campaign for Pavanne novels: 'An interesting diversion for women who don't need one'. Apart from leg-warmers, the New Women who are publicized as the market for the 'New Romance' are introduced by such cryptic phrases as *'Can an Estate Agent Fall in Love?'* – amplified as follows: 'Jane Forsyth is a partner in a rapidly expanding firm of Estate Agents. What she doesn't know about the property business doesn't make money. Like any successful businesswoman, Jane knows how to separate business from pleasure. One of her occasional pleasures is reading a Pavanne Novel. She knows that after a hard day's work she can afford a little romantic speculation.' The same applies to Carol Dunn (Borough Councillor), Angela Welch (barrister) and Sue Davey (fashion executive). Reassuring, to know that today's hard-headed woman still needs a little Romantic icing on the plain cake of working life.

What is it, then, that the successful New Woman *reads?* Pavanne launches with four novels. Pamela Street's *Light of Evening* announces itself thus: 'He was impossible. Impossible and irresistible. Sophie chose to go where he led – to London, to Chicago, to the South of France. All she had to do was *pay the price* of choosing, to give up her home, husband and child for another man . . .'. This was described in one review (the *Daily Mail* – Leg-Warmers Anonymous) as 'a deeply feminine blueprint of woman's eternal dilemma'. Then there's *Columbine* by Raymond Kennedy – 'She waited at the brink of womanhood, when he came back from war looking for life and love. He brought her over the threshold of sexuality, and then he taught her the *pain of love* . . .'. *An Easter Egg Hunt* is a clever mystery story set in an Edwardian girls' school: 'On Easter Sunday the girls of the select academy were to go on an Easter Egg hunt. One of them never returned. She was seventeen and deeply in love with an airman already *marked down to die* . . .' (all my italics). 'A brooding, haunting, highly-charged story', says *Cosmo,* another leg-warming ally. The fourth title is *Pas de Deux* by Olivier Beer, a modern Bonnie and Clyde story of two young criminals doomed to die. Despite translation, this is the only one of the four to show some delight in language, with the sense that writing is anything more than a vehicle for tales which grab your emotions by the short hairs and drag them through plots that to me, at least, are the literary equivalent of pornography. For these novels are structured so as to make reading them rather like trying to peel one's eyes from an erotic photograph.

This quality is by no means new in 'women's romance'. The *Woman's Weekly* library, the slushy paperbacks at stations, are part of a tradition that runs from the eighteenth century 'sentimental novel' (which Sterne parodied in *A Sentimental Journey*) – novels full of tears, guilt, pity and remorse – through the Gothic novels and fantasies where the monster of sexuality rears its head from creaking chains in castles and wild, deserted places. There is a certain avid, secret, hungry quality with which one reads both these and many other kinds of novel, a quality which seems to me not unlike that which gives the pornographic its forbidden thrill.

And it turns out that, despite being plugged as different, new and modern, Pavanne books share with their down-market sisters, and their historical (Gothic, sentimental) grandmothers, one key fact: the demon which haunts them, the monster in the wings which gives the frisson of danger in each novel, is no less than *women's* sexuality! We have the seventeen-year-old girl in *Pas de Deux* who eggs her boyfriend on to crime, finishing with a bloody death. Seen through the eyes of the first-person narrator, her young lover, she appears only as amazingly beautiful, and more ruthless than the boy, like the women in countless 'films noirs'. In *Light of Evening* there is the middle-aged married woman whose sexual passion, 'awakened' by an older artist, pulls her into what is depicted as a humiliating relationship. She is hooked on it like a drug, becomes an alcoholic and still clings to her lover because their sexual passion is so consuming. When she's away from him, 'despite her anger and indignation . . . she longed to *be made love to* again' (my italics). Not once do the couple make love together, nor does she make love to him – he does it to her, and she's addicted. Then there is *Columbine*, written, like *Pas de Deux*, from the man's point of view, about a young World War 2 veteran who loves the girl-next-door, a promiscuous thirteen-year-old ('unconscious of her own deepest impulses') whose sexuality arouses scandal and shame, and

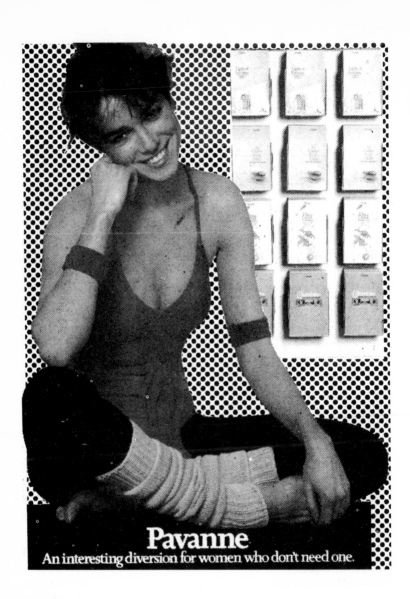

Pavanne
An interesting diversion for women who don't need one.

34

results in her virtual rape. Finally, in *An Easter Egg Hunt* the horror and scandal are accounted for by the period setting, as a schoolgirl in World War 1 who becomes pregnant by an airman, disappears – a mystery which is solved as we learn that she died after an abortion performed by a doctor who has a strange and sinister passion for her himself.

There is very little actual 'sex' in these novels, yet they are haunted by sex as the out-of-bounds, and the thread which pulls you through them is one twisted out of curiosity, repulsion and fear. The impact of, say, a violent kiss, in an old-fashioned 'women's paperback', is simply transferred onto sexuality at a deeper level. The limits of the out-of-bounds have changed, but exactly the same thrill is manufactured by forays across them. The Pavanne blurb rambles on about 'scandal and humiliation' with great accuracy. These are novels full of punishment, humiliation and shame (as if we needed more of those things). Their general message is that sex is *fatal* for women – literally, in most cases – but still exciting.

And these 'deeply feminine' thrills are purchasable, from stands that make them look exactly like packets of tights (don't let the leg-warmers fool you). Evidently, we busy career women need to buy our tremors of soft-core self-punishment as conveniently as panti-hose, packaging it into our busy days, occasionally taking time off to savour the *frisson* of that dangerous monster we carry inside – our sexual feelings. They could be our downfall, as these books show, but we know how to 'separate business from pleasure', as the ad says: reading novels like these both compensates for, and justifies, suppressing our sexuality in order to succeed in a man's world. Can a journalist fall in love? Well, let me just say that I was paid to read these books, and rarely have business and pleasure felt further apart.

(City Limits, 1982)

SEX BY NUMBERS

Despite all our troubles, we live in a time of great discovery. 'In each of the last four decades, a book has been published that has greatly altered our understanding and knowledge about human sexuality. The pioneering works of Kinsey, Masters and Johnson, and Hite are about to be succeeded in the 1980s by *The G Spot and Other Recent Discoveries about Human Sexuality*. Never before have the facts been explained so thoroughly and convincingly, within the context of other sexual discoveries throughout history. Scientific and statistical evidence is included to substantiate the pioneering work of the authors . . . Bound to be widely read and hotly argued, *The G Spot* is the perfect guide for millions of people who want to explore further the pleasures of their sexuality'.

So runs the jacket blurb; and inside, authors Ladas, Whipple and Perry's own message: 'This book is about important newly discovered facts that are crucial to our understanding of how human beings function sexually. We believe that the information presented here can be used to help millions of women and men lead more pleasurable and satisfying lives and avoid a good deal of unnecessary suffering and frustration'. In this one field, at least, the endless red carpet of Progress unfurls faster than we can run down it, discovery succeeding discovery on the path to true 'understanding and knowledge about human sexuality'. For those of us who have grown up under the artificial light of positivism, believing that science and society march forward into the future hand in hand like the children in the Start-Rite ad, there is still one area where technology, medicine and statistical logic can offer riches, in the midst of general devastation. That area is physically small, but in the alchemy of science, its power and effects are magically limitless. It appears to be on the one hand, a small area the size of a bean located on the inside wall of the vagina, and also, simultaneously, 'sexuality', that mystical substance denoted by a word which only came into existence in the nineteenth century.

That access to 'human sexuality' should be afforded through such a small and specific spot is a mystery to unravel later. But as long as we understand 'sexuality' to be as old as the hills, and only our understanding and knowledge of it to be new, we miss the point that in the modern era, 'sexuality' has been set up, precisely *to be understood*. The relatively recent use of the word itself shows that it is a particular *concept* of sex which characterizes our own time, not the revealing of sex itself, which, after all, has always been known to people.

For what is so interesting about these twentieth century 'discoveries' about sexuality – a context in which this new book quite rightly places itself – is not the actual findings, which are always either statistical or clinical, but the evangelical nature of their de-mystifying, in fact the belief that they are indeed de-mystifying anything. A mystique is created in the very act of ostentatiously knocking it down. A glance over the last few issues of *Cosmopolitan* – a key product of this era – shows this most simply: 'sex myths exploded' (what myths?); 'sex – the new realism' (what was the old idealism?); 'How I stopped worrying and put sex into perspective' (*were* you worrying?); and finally, the ultimate modern dictate, 'be true to your own sexuality'. The real point about this endless, obsessive speech about sex is that it claims over and over again to destroy some previous notion, it is a knowledge that parades a cast-off ignorance before it like a shadow. Ours is a society which speaks insistently of what it doesn't speak of, relentlessly finding things that no-one had lost in the first place.

And the territory of the great march forward into sexual knowledge always seems to be the *female* body. It is *our* bodies the pioneers search, for clues into 'the understanding of human sexuality' – yet another case of 'they've got it, she wears it'. Far more revealing than anything *The G Spot* could reveal about our bodies, is the claim that 'these findings constitute an important step in demystifying Freud's "dark continent", which is not quite as dark as it was when he coined that phrase in connection with female sexuality one hundred years ago. But much more research remains to be done'. The missionary zeal with which this colonization of the dark continent takes place is one which holds up a light, precisely to reveal darkness; an empire on which the sun never sets, but is always rising. Maybe the dark continent is no longer 'quite as dark' – but there can be no slacking, 'much more remains to be done'.

So what are the 'new facts' that further this cause? The G spot itself, called after Ernst Gräfenberg who 'discovered' it in the '40s, is a small, invisible area of sexual sensitivity 'usually located about halfway between the back of the pubic bone and the front of the cervix . . . the exact size and location vary. It lies deep within the vaginal wall . . .' – like the Sleeping Beauty, waiting for Prince Science to awaken it from centuries of oblivion. 'The clitoris, located outside the body, is easy for every woman to discover and enjoy by herself. The G spot, located inside the anterior wall of the vagina, is more difficult for a woman to find on her own.'

Here is a difficulty we did not know we had until Knowledge handed it to us. But why now? The G spot was not, in fact, 'discovered' but only cashed in on, in the 1980s.

The particular significance it acquires in this book comes from its association with the 'dramatic discovery' of female ejaculation. The G spot is found to be the equivalent of the male prostate gland, and its stimulation produces an ejaculation similar to men's. The excitement at finding this analogy also hands us something we might not have felt – that we were missing something because we were different. Now we know we are up to scratch: we have an equivalent for the penis (the clitoris) and the prostate (the G spot) and we can also come like the boys. The relief of the specialists at finding these precise analogies measures the unease, perhaps, aroused by sexual *difference*. But for women, the endless reassurances which accompany each 'discovery' are merely the giftwrapping for more anxieties. It is *perfectly normal* to ejaculate a quantity of fluid through the urethra on orgasm – but what if one *doesn't?* The sexual tasks pile up like homework on a Sunday night.

The authors claim that 'the G spot is what specifically frees us from the either/or thinking of past decades', i.e. the clitoral vs. vaginal orgasm debate. They begin the book with a tour through Freud, Kinsey, Masters and Johnson and others, leading up to their own discoveries as if on an inevitable escalator to enlightenment: 'These four discoveries, the Grafenberg spot, female ejaculation, the importance of pelvic muscle tone and the continuum of orgasmic response, unify the findings of the Freudians and other sex researchers into an understandable and consistent whole. Our dilemma is resolved. We now have a new synthesis that validates the experience of both vaginal and clitoral orgasm.' They parade their work as the solution to an enormous dilemma. (*Our* dilemma?) But why was it a dilemma in the first place? In claiming to solve it, they actually confirm that there *was* a problem to be solved – the 'problem' of the female orgasm. Although *The G Spot* is so superbly liberal in allowing both sides of the debate to be true, it also confirms the categories of clitoral/vaginal orgasm even further than before, with its diagrams showing the difference between the 'Tenting' (clitoral) and 'A-Frame' (G spot) effects – which make one's vagina sound like a campsite.

The point about the clitoral/vaginal argument, whether seen from one side or the other, or 'both', is that it presupposes an incredible faith in the truth of scientific categorization – a truth which one would think would be questionable simply on account of its so frequent updating. It is a strange assumption that we need our experience of orgasm validated by research, as if it was not valid on its own. Clearly there is an enormous range of sexual experiences, and obviously sex feels different having something inside you. *The G Spot* mistakes trying to name the wheel for inventing it.

This is exemplified in the opening chapter, where the authors remind us that Kinsey *et al* 'certainly brought into the open a whole range of human behaviour that had previously been discussed only in whispers behind closed doors, if at all.' Oh, how they love those whispers, which confirm their own imagined shout! Those closed doors, which they believe they are the first to open. But historically, this is nonsense. Sexual theories were in the market-place long before the twentieth century. A popular sex manual, bizarrely titled *Aristotle's Masterpiece,* which ran through hundreds of editions over the sixteenth to eighteenth centuries, was most graphic about the identification of the clitoris as 'the seat of venereal pleasure' in women, and the female capacity for multiple orgasms; and such works as this were, as an eighteenth century observer wrote, 'sold openly on every stall'.

No, what is modern is the idea that sex is such an explosive subject. 'Three times in this century, great pioneers in the field of human sexuality have shocked, informed and transformed our world. The people responsible for these *seismic changes* are Sigmund Freud, Alfred Kinsey and the team of Masters and Johnson' (my italics).

And this seismic shock – 'tenting', perhaps – is nothing to the global, 'A–Frame' orgasm triggered by *The G Spot.* Its main selling point is not, in fact, its discoveries, but the controversy and violent storms it claims already to have aroused. The publishers themselves suggest that the truth of the argument is far less important than its impact: 'As expected, publication of *The G Spot* has *set off fireworks* amongst sexologists – some wholeheartedly agree with the existence of the spot, whilst others fault the authors' research. One thing however is quite certain – no other book has ever prompted such a response from the public' (my italics).

The repeated emphasis on this flood of response carries overtones not only of sexual eruption, but also of the Confessional, in which 'hundreds of case histories and personal testimonies' pour through the grille to our high priests of modern sexuality. Sex and confession have always been intimately linked, but with *The G Spot* this is hardly metaphorical: one of the authors, John D. Perry, MDiv, PhD is 'an ordained minister, psychologist and sexologist, specializing in vaginal myography and other innovative applications of bio-feedback, the inventor of the Electronic Perineometer which measures the tone and health of pelvic muscles.' The chapter devoted to Minister Perry's device, headed 'The Importance of Healthy Pelvic Muscles', suggests it is a moral duty to keep your pubococcygeus muscles in tip-top shape through constant vigilance: 'You can encourage yourself by placing some kind of reminder where you will see it. For example, affix a brightly coloured dot to your briefcase, the telephone, the refrigerator, a clock or lamp. Every time you see the dot, contract your PC muscle several times.' The religious energies once used to suppress the sexual are now conveniently, but equally obsessively, channelled into it. There is the case history of an extremely religious woman whose husband 'threatened to get a divorce if she did not get medical help for her weak muscles.

According to the therapist "she was the best patient I ever treated. She was literally motivated by the fear of Hell and Damnation . . . She practised like mad . . .".'

The peculiar machines for measuring the strength of your contractions look like a dog-bone attached to a battery charger and are on mail order at the end of the book, with the footnote: ' *"Personal Perineometer"* (patents pending) is a trademark of Health Technology Inc . . . *"Femtone Isometric Vaginal Exerciser"* is a trademark of J & L Feminine Research Center . . . *"The Vagette 76"* is a trademark of Myodynamics Inc . . .' and so on. There is money to be made from pelvic contractions.

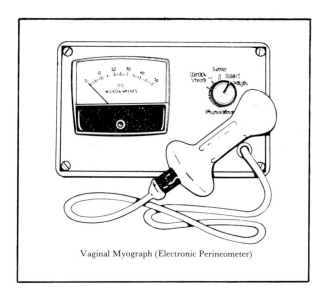

Vaginal Myograph (Electronic Perineometer)

The obsession with sex as health follows directly from Reich and his excessive belief in the social power of orgasms. But it takes on a sinister edge here, since 'undiagnosed chronic pelvic tension . . . can also contribute to more serious problems' like, guess what, cancer, the punishment of our time for a failure to THINK POSITIVE. Your *attitude* is all-important: *The G Spot* bullies with the voice of a games mistress or brisk nurse. It prescribes Sexual Healing as if it were a form of Savlon.

For the most striking aspect of the whole G spot enterprise (and others like it) is the way it manages to de-eroticize sex. Our bodies become a form of fruit-machine, to be played on for pleasures: women can have different kinds of orgasms, multiple orgasms, plateaux, climaxes, ejaculations, you name it. But how about desire? – without which the G spot is as useful as a hole in the head, and which, equally, can turn the nape of your neck or the back of your hand into a sexual explosion. But it is always as if men have desire, women have 'pleasure' – usually 'given' by a man. You can bet that hordes of heterosexual couples will be up all night searching for *her* G spot, not *his* prostate gland (which the book also locates).

Underlying the very earnestness of this search are two mistakes. The first is a tendency to overestimate the power of 'sexuality', which in recent times has taken on a pseudo-radical role. In modern jargon sexuality 'frees' us; it has become part of a discourse of 'liberation' which makes repression, rather than oppression, the enemy of human happiness. But is 'sexuality' really the arena in which our well-being is determined in the power-structure of modern societies? And if indeed we overestimate its power, what effect does this have? What is the function of an ideology that keeps everyone looking for the meaning of life up their own or someone else's vagina?

But the second mistake is the assumption that 'sexuality' can be conjured up through anatomical locations: the G spot plays the part of Aladdin's lamp, with female sexuality as the genie. The whole drive of books like this, and the articles which reinforce them, is one that simultaneously sets up 'sexuality' as unfathomable, while purporting to fathom it through de-sexualized clinical information. When will they stop searching our bodies for new sources of pleasure, and allow us desire?

(First published as 'Seeing Spots',
City Limits, 1983)

IT'S DIFFERENT FOR GIRLS

In this era of Boy George and Grace Jones, when jeans and tracksuits are normal wear for both men and women, it might seem that we are moving towards a unisex style culture. And drag, the deliberate dressing-up as the opposite sex, might appear as part of that same liberation from sex roles which feminists have demanded for years, and sometimes pursued through dress, in trousers and dungarees, short hair-cuts and bomber jackets. Not that this is exactly a form of drag, but rather the recognition of genderized dress and body image as being in some way a symbol of the workings of power in a society in which power is invested in the male sex. But it is precisely this imbalance of power in both sexual relations and society at large, which makes the equation of men dressing up as women, and women dressing up as men, less even than it might seem: drag is not a simply reversible phenomenon.

To understand the real social/sexual meanings of drag, and of body images in general, I would argue that you must look not so much at the *men* who dress as women, or the *women* who dress as men, but at the 'feminine' or 'masculine' characteristics they adopt, and the values placed on these, no matter who 'wears' them. This means separating actual gender (male/female) from the 'masculine' and 'feminine' characteristics that either sex can adopt or play down, worship or parody. The feminine is usually characterized by breasts, hips and curves, and the masculine by a taller, leaner shape, flat stomach, hard thighs. But these are not just caricatures: men and women *are* for the most part built differently. Women inevitably have 'tummies' which are different from men's since they house an entire organ men don't have – the womb. Women biologically have more subcutaneous fat than men, and differently distributed: they have wider hips and, obviously enough, breasts. Of course there is one further, fundamental difference in body shape between the sexes: men have the appendage of the penis. But this crucial difference is revealingly absent from the style language of drag and sex role games.

Instead, it is big tits, fat tummies, wobbly hips and elaborate hair-dos that feature most widely in popular images of drag. And they are usually a joke. 'Feminine' characteristics are parodied by Hinge and Bracket, Dame Edna Everage, and other well-known female impersonators. The *man* in each case isn't being undermined: *female* characteristics, and by implication *women, are*. There is nothing inherently radical about men dressing as women. After all, under all those skirts and stuffed bras there's still a perfectly safe penis. Men can have their cake and eat it, in this respect, since they don't actually have to undermine their own sexual characteristics in order to adopt and undermine women's. And we have yet to see a female comic stuff a sock in her trousers and waggle it at crowded studio audiences to roars of laughter.

Why is it that female body characteristics are supposedly funny, while male ones patently aren't? On the social level, as long as women are less powerful than men and treated as inferior, the characteristics of maleness will probably be valued more highly, and taken more seriously than those of femaleness. But another aspect of the relentless, almost hysterical joking about women's bodies, tits, bums etc., is perhaps the *unease* aroused by femininity, by the fact that women do indeed lack that most serious of assets, the penis. As the song says, It's Different for Girls: and girls are *different*. They are the Other, the departure from the norm. The threat posed to a value system based on possession of the penis, by the very possibility of its absence, is enormous. Women's bodies frequently provoke fear in men; and joking can diffuse fear, while men dressing as women can appear to bridge the frightening gap of sexual difference. After all, if men can do it (be women) there's nothing to it!

If men taking a female appearance helps to disperse that uneasy sense of the'Other', the un-male, what can *women* do to help further dismantle the threat posed by their sex? Not look like women, of course. Here I am *not* referring to those women mentioned above who dress outside traditional 'feminine' stereotypes to avoid being looked on as sexually available, weak or inferior. Certainly this is part of the same language of body image and power; but an important part of the women's liberation project has always been to *affirm* the female body, and allow its natural shape – different for each woman – to appear unfettered by corsetry and not pushed by high heels etc into the exaggerated postures which turn the female form into almost a parody of itself (as happens with Marilyn Monroe in *Some Like It Hot*). In our society fake breasts on male comedians are funny, but real breasts on women who don't wear bras, or breastfeed in public, are less acceptable. The point for many feminists is not to resist looking like *women* – it is to resist looking like a fashion-plate model, or rather, to come to terms with *not* looking like one.

And the fashion images that we inevitably compare ourselves with (to be found lacking!) are of figures that resemble not so much women, as *boys*. For many decades the desirable shape held out through fashion photos and adverts has been that of a lean, tall, flat-tummied boy – leggy, tight-bummed, curve-less. Endless boyish models with tousled hair, long thin legs and no hips pout at us from every magazine, their armpits and so-called bikini areas immaculately hairless, a total denial of adult women's sexual qualities. Most of these models are women who look boyish, but an extreme example of this phenomenon is the model Tula (who appears in the Smirnoff Loch Ness advert). Tula is actually a man, Barry Cossey, who has undergone a sex change. This of course involved a change-around of basic organs; yet the totally hard, flat stomach and lean torso, the spare bone structure and long limbs, look more male than female. Tula as a model is a blueprint for women. The fact that her body started off male seems an ironic comment not on sex-changes or Tula herself, but on the whole body image industry, modelling, photography, fashion, which can sell us the male form as the ideal for *females*.

The desirable shape for a woman, then, is that of a boy. This is easier for some women to achieve than others; thousands of anorexic women believe their already emaciated thighs are too fat, their breasts too big, their tummies too round – their self-image wildly distorted in a grotesque parody of the boy-fashion phenomenon. Yet there is nothing funny about *this* parody; it is the comic figures who *have* the wobbly bustlines that are amusing. So it seems that the 'silliest', least valued shape for either men *or* women, is 'womanly': and the most fashionable, most valued shape for both sexes, 'boyish'.

Comedy aside, *'unisex'* invariably means boyish. In style – Grace Jones' sharp, lean look is a trendsetter for both women and men. Yes, she's a woman, but it is the *masculinity* of this style that makes it smart. In clothes – it means trousers, jeans, suits, sweatshirts, *male* sportsgear (shorts, *not* tennis-skirts!). In shape – many of the clothes currently fashionable, including sportsgear, have a flattening effect; loose, flat tops conceal breasts, the bosomy look is definitely out. Meanwhile, jeans advertising has concentrated heavily on bottoms; with pictures of male and female bodies alike poured into skin-tight jeans that mould sexually

indistinguishable small, tight bums. True, a new Levi's campaign now sells jeans specially fitted for girls; but the point is, they are specially fitted for girls to *have* that skin-tight, boyish-bum *look*. The shift in public imagery and style from breasts to bottoms is surely a move away from the 'ideal woman' male fantasy towards the (equally male) fantasy of the 'ideal boy'. And while this mainly involves a shift in imagery, there is a similar trend in actual sports and 'training', with famous examples like Lisa Lyon whose body-building producing a taut, muscular physique, earns her inclusion among Robert Mapplethorpe's mainly homosexual, muscle-bound, hard-bodied male subjects. This is not to criticize the project in itself; but to draw attention to the high fashion value placed on eliminating female body characteristics.

So how about recent examples of men dressing as *women,* not in the Hinge and Bracket vein, but in more serious or stylish form? There is Boy George, slightly pudgy of face, slightly prissy of gesture – feminine, rather than masculine in image. But however girlish he acts, George's title is a crucial and revealing part of his charm. Thousands of teenage girls both worship, *and* try to look like Boy George; suggesting a wish to *be* the object of desire, as much as to 'have' him, in other words, to be the recipient rather than the initiator of passions. For what is perhaps most interesting about Boy George is his much proclaimed *celibacy*. In both fan-mags and the popular press, George's lack of interest in a sex-life has been widely publicized. This allows his sexuality to remain completely ambiguous, since no-one seems to know whether his partner would be male or female, if he had one. His pudginess is, in fact, rather reminiscent of the way people sometimes get when they don't have sex. So in a curious way, Boy George seems less bi-sexual, than a-sexual; he has that smooth, hairless, rounded quality almost like a baby, which can be very appealing to those who like the object of their desire passive and unthreatening. There is a dimension to the sexual ambiguity fashion which is actually a way of avoiding sexuality. After all, a cute girlish boy, or a lean, tomboyish girl, aren't actually meant to have *active* sexual feelings. (The fact that children do, of course, is another matter). If you present yourself as pre-sexual, you may arouse desire in others, but you can also absolve yourself of the responsibility for it. The currently fashionable boy/girl figure is bland and impassive, seeming not to have a sexuality of its own but to offer itself as a peg for the fantasies of others. Unenergetic, limp, even, Boy George is not shocking or exciting in his androgeny (as, for example, Mick Jagger or David Bowie always have been); he is, ultimately, supremely *safe.*

A very different contemporary example of man-as-woman, hailed as radical by many people, was Dustin Hoffman in *Tootsie.* After all, the film was 'about' sexism; as 'Dorothy', the Dustin Hoffman character Michael Dorsey finds that he is treated as inferior and subjected to sexual harassment and names like 'tootsie'. But it is Michael/Dorothy who leads the silly, flighty, timorous women of the film in the fight against sexism: showing that men not only make the best women, they make the best *feminists* (!). And of course the joke, and the whole point, is that 'Dorothy' isn't a woman, he is a man: Michael is simply an out-of-work actor trying for the part that his girlfriend has been too useless to get. Anyone, it seems, can be a woman, but not everyone can be as motivated and courageous as a man. For there is not one real woman in the film who is shown to be nearly as fine as 'Dorothy', there is only the 'silly, gawky' girlfriend (whom, as a man, Michael treats appallingly) and the 'cute, feather-brained' second girlfriend whom Michael is paired with at the end.

The values of 'masculine' and 'feminine' in style are ultimately bound up with the values placed on actual male and female roles in social and sexual life. Taking on the clothes or shape of the opposite sex may be individually liberating for anyone who wants to play with stereotypes and 'escape' their conventional gender image: yet as long as the value of male/female is imbalanced, even those 'transgressions' remain within a convention of a different kind. To play with the language of gender is not to escape it, merely to detach it from the sex of the 'wearer'. As I said: the day I see a female comic on a family TV show with a padded penis (what a joke! One of *those!* Isn't it wobbly, ha ha! Just like my father-in-law's! Get a load of *that!* etc) I will believe in the radical equality of unisex and drag.

(City Limits, 1984)

MISS PIGGY'S GUIDE TO LIFE

Whatever the drive is that keeps thousands of women –including myself – buying magazines like *Cosmopolitan* every month, it has more to do with improvement than entertainment. Why else should one curl up after a hard day at work with a publication which tells you to 'Shape up for summer – NOW', 'Tune into that TOP job', 'WORK off that extra weight' and 'Don't daydream, dare to SUC-CEED'? This pep-talk format is a key feature of selling the magazine even before it is opened. 'Change your face in a day, Slip into a loose T-Shirt, Learn a language this summer', insists just one corner of a recent *Cosmo* cover, and every month brings still *more* pressing ways for the *Cosmo* Girl to improve her Health, her Wealth and her Self.

However urgent and immediate these exhortations may *sound,* the subject-matter of the articles they refer to changes very little over any stretch of time. Features may appear contradictory – 'Face up to the New Sexual Free-dom', 'Chastity – the New Challenge' – but fundamentally they revolve around the same issues of work, sex, emotional life, and feminism. Many of the articles are interesting and informative, and the overall suggestion that women take their working lives seriously is very valuable, as is much of the advice on relationships and emotional problems. But whatever the content, the mode of address is the same: check this, aim for that, start this, stop that – the omnipresent *imperative.*

The flip-side of this is the searching *question:* How do YOU look at work? Are you capable of a normal relationship? Are you fit for sex? Can your marriage survive a baby? Are you as liberated as you think? These basic structures of question and command offer to reveal, on the one hand, what you are like, and on the other, how to be *better.* There are plenty of quizzes to help you find what kind of person you are before embarking on the royal road to improvement: 'How inhibited are you?' 'Is your relationship on the rocks?' 'Are you programmed for success?' 'Are you serious about sex?' and 'Check your happiness quotient'. Underlying all this are two somewhat confused premises: first, that you can find out your true nature (are you a dreamer or an achiever? Do you prefer your sex friendly or funky?) – second, that you can change it if you try hard enough. The fuel that keeps these magazines selling, when their material is so fundamentally repetitive, is partly the appetite to *discover* the self (primarily through sexuality) and simultaneously, the search for a *new* self; both quests which are inherently unending. Specific articles, of course, often do give precise and concrete help or understanding; it is the *drive* that keeps one reading (and buying) which is so insatiable. Fulfilment, for modern woman, seems to be fixed just around the corner, always an article away, on the other side of some giant 'SHOULD'.

In this feminine world of deferred gratification, where people slim their way to fitness and plan their way to the top, *Miss Piggy's Guide to Life* is most refreshing: for here you can have your discipline and eat it too. Miss Piggy, for example, *snacks* her way to slimness: 'The trouble with so many diets is that they ignore a very simple fact: people eat because they are hungry, and they overeat because they are extremely hungry.' The obvious solution is to 'snack your way to the weight you desire *by nipping hunger in the bud whenever it appears.'* Thus diet of the day for Wednesday runs,

3.34 Two cookies
4.14 One more cookie
4.51 Small handful of peanuts
5.17 Slightly larger handful of peanuts
5.44 The rest of the peanuts
6.11 Crackers with cheese dip
6.32 Breadstick with cheese dip
6.45 Cheese chips with cheese dip
7.10 Small slice of cake from piece left in icebox
7.26 Remainder of cake (really, it is silly to have such a small piece of cake on a big plate taking up so much room) . . .

. . . and so on. And the total calorie count comes to merely 'a fraction of your usual dinner intake!'.

Within precisely the *Cosmo* format of *rules, lists* and *tasks,* Miss Piggy lets the desire for immediate gratification run riot. From Fashion to Finance, she challenges all the prudent wisdom of the *Cosmo* Girl: 'Many people think money is something to be set aside for a rainy day. But honestly, how much money do you really *need* for a dozen or so hours of inclement weather?' Her Beauty hints are unique in their understanding of the essential nutrients one's body needs, as in this special Style-and-Smile Hair Conditioning Recipe:

1. Heat the milk, sugar, and chocolate, beat in the yolks, then whip in the vanilla and the egg whites. Place in the oven on very low heat.
2. Go out and have your hair done.
3. Come home, remove mixture from oven, cover lightly with whipped cream, and eat.

On the other hand, her dinner recipes involve a step-by-step guide to phoning the nearest take-away.

Miss Piggy's *style* of advice, based on following her own footsteps to fame and success, is extremely close to that of Helen Gurley Brown, author of *Sex and the Single Girl* and founder of *Cosmopolitan*. If Miss Piggy's focus on food seems a little excessive, it might be seen in the light of this quote from Helen Gurley Brown's latest guide to every-thing, *Having It All:* 'After someone has made love to you with skill and grace, having an orgasm is a way of saying you enjoyed yourself, even as you compliment a host on a wonderful spinach quiche.' It is no coincidence that food finds its way to the 'Sex' section of *Having It All,* it is so conspicuously absent from its own section – called, pointed-ly, 'Diet' – where fighting back the urge to indulge oneself is the major theme. (Ditto for 'Exercise', 'Face' and 'Body'.) No wonder the poor suppressed quiche pops up in the orgasm department.

But even in sex, you are *still* not to follow your own whims: what do you do 'When He Wants To Make Love and You Don't?' – *'Do it anyway'*. 'Sometimes The Scene Makes Up For The Man': *'ultradiscriminating girls'* fail to realize that one can 'have a *nice sexual experience* just because the scene is *magical* and the man *acceptable.'* 'Should You Do Anything You Don't Like During Sex?' *Yes,* provided it isn't actually 'perverted'. The ultimate aim of all this putting up with things in bed, is a good relationship with your man, and a well-stocked store of experience for yourself.

What Miss Piggy subverts is exactly this notion of *investment* – a feature of capitalism which pervades all women's magazines. What you put in, you will one day get out; starving yourself/working hard/not letting HIM know how you feel, and so on, will pay off dividends in the long run, or at least, *later*. Miss Piggy's attack on this most bourgeois – and protestant – of principles, extends far beyond her acute observation that money can rot with time if not used, and that too much money staying in your purse can be a fire hazard. Her etiquette guide is most expressive:

*What do you do if a man you like, and who likes you, still
wants to see other women?*
– Although this is by definition a somewhat emotional
matter, you should approach it in a calm, reasonable,
mature way. What I would do is calmly, reasonably, and
maturely explain to him that if he values his life, he should
change his behaviour.

Her calculation of the calories burnt by lifting candies to the
mouth, picking up heavy cups of hot chocolate, and other
daily tasks, seems to make all other exercise plans redun-
dant. And no longer need anyone feel a failure at that most
crucial of modern female accomplishments, lightweight
travelling; Miss Piggy's basic rule is: 'When in doubt, *pack
it.*'

In Miss Piggy's world, the present makes absolutely no
sacrifices to the future. There is no reason to deny oneself
anything. Comic though it is, the effect of reading her *Guide*
is liberating in a way reminiscent of passages in Susie
Orbach's *Fat is a Feminist Issue,* where suggested therapy for
overeaters is to fantasize buying large quantities of their
favourite food, and then to be told that they can have any of
it, in any amount, anytime they want. *Fat is a Feminist Issue*
is a deadly serious book; and not just about food, which is
merely the *symbol* of need and denial for many women. *Miss
Piggy's Guide to Life,* by contrast, is uproariously funny,
because total *indulgence* is couched in the language of
strictness. It simultaneously fulfils that peculiar desire for
someone to *tell* us what to do and how to do it, while
justifying, through complex twists of logic, doing whatever
you would most feel like anyway.

But what is so interesting is the wish to be 'told' in the first
place; which brings us back to *Cosmo.* Why is it that women
respond so readily to the idea that we *ought* to do anything?
The flip-side of this 'ought' is, precisely, the 'naughty'; a
phenomenon ruthlessly exploited by food advertisements of
every kind. Behind every enjoyment lurks an all-purpose

YOU CAN BE A LITTLE NAUGHTY ON SATURDAY NIGHT. IF YOU'VE BEEN A GOOD GIRL ALL WEEK.

Did you realise that by the time you've eaten just a third of a pack of Outline, instead of butter, you can enjoy a Saturday night celebration with the calories you've already saved?

Well, you can. Because a 250-gram pack of butter or margarine has 1,860 calories, whereas a 250-gram pack of Outline has only 930 calories.

So with Outline as part of your calorie-controlled diet you can either save the calories, or spend them on a real treat. The choice is up to you. **DIET. WHAT DIET?**

guilt – until guilt itself becomes a form of enjoyment. But Miss Piggy has the number of female masochism, even in its most literary forms (where it often appears today under the guise of feminism, even from the 'feminist' press). So the last word on her *Guide to Life* must go to my heroine herself. 'If an ill-informed bookseller attempted to convince me to substitute for it some flossy novel about sad people in big houses by a woman with three names, I would reject it politely but without hesitation. "Take back your flossy novel about sad people in big houses by a woman with three names" I would insist, indicating with a quick movement of my hand in what contempt I held such trash. And then, helping him from the floor, I would ask him in the nicest possible way to wrap up my *Guide* in some pretty gift paper'.

If only Miss Piggy would start a magazine.

(1984)

PICTURE THIS

All I want is a room with a view
a sight worth seeing
a vision of you
All I want is a room with a view

I will give you my finest hour
the one I spent
watching you shower
I will give you my finest hour

All I want is a photo in my wallet
a small remembrance
of something more solid
All I want is a picture of you

Picture this – a day in December
Picture this – freezing cold weather
You got clouds on your lids and you'd be on the skids
    if it weren't for your job at the garage
    if you could only,
Picture this – a sky full of thunder
Picture this – my telephone number
One and one is what I'm telling you

All I want is 20–20 vision
a total portrait
with no omissions
All I want is a vision of you

If you can . . .

Picture this – a day in December
Picture this – freezing cold weather
You got clouds on your lids and you'd be on the skids
    if it weren't for your job at the garage
    if you could only,
Picture this – a sky full of thunder
Picture this – my telephone number
One and one is what I'm telling you

get a pocket computer
try to do what ya used to do.

D. Harry/C. Stein/J. Destri, *'Picture This'*
(for Blondie)

. . . BUT I KNOW WHAT I LIKE
The Function of 'Art' in Advertising

Advertising is part of a system which not only sells us *things* – it sells us 'choices': or, to be more precise, sells us the idea that we are 'free' to 'choose' *between* things. To nourish this 'freedom' advertising must, like other key ideological forms, cover its own tracks and assert that these choices are the result of personal taste. As a contemporary advert puts it: *'One instinctively knows when something is right'*. In our society 'high' and 'low' cultural forms share the same speech: for this pompous phrase could equally have leapt straight from the mouth of that most instinctive bourgeois character The Artist.

Unlike advertising, Art has a reputation for being above things vulgar and mercenary, a form eternal rather than social, whose appreciation springs from the discerning heart, not the cultural background. This ethereal notion can be brought down with a bump by the merest glimpse, on the one hand at the Art market, distinguished from other fields of commercial gain only by the intriguing fact that it successfully deals in the 'priceless', and on the other hand, at that equally effective cultural economy whereby anything that too many people like is rapidly devalued as 'Art'. Classical music which makes it onto '100 Favourites' LPs becomes scorned by 'serious' music lovers; reproductions even of 'valued' paintings, like Van Gogh's 'Sunflowers', disappear from the walls of the cognoscenti when they become widely enough loved to be sold in Woolworth's.

It is on this 'cultural economy' that advertising feeds its endless appetite for social values. Ads are in the business not of creating, but of re-cycling social categories, relying on systems of value already in existence as sources for the 'auras', at once intangible and precise, which must be associated with the goods for sale. Any system which is already structured in terms of up-market and down-market is especially useful, the more so if it has a high investment in denying its own workings. Advertising pitches its products at specific social classes (carefully graded from A to E) yet, as with Art, choice and taste must appear as personal attributes of the individual. So 'Art' is a particularly appropriate system for ads: while appearing to be 'above' social distinctions, it provides a distinct set of social codes which we all understand.

For what is interesting is the degree of agreement at both ends of the social scale as to what 'Art' is. Art is felt to be 'difficult', its meaning not accessible by mere everyday use of the perceptive faculties. It is something which the great majority of people feel is somehow above them, out of reach and beyond their grasp. This perfectly mirrors the opinion of those select few who can be assured of their good taste simply by its exclusiveness.

It is in the light of these implications that the Benson and Hedges campaign appears in its full brilliance. Usually seen as an application of surrealist style to advertising, it is in fact much more: an application of social assumptions about class, taste and Art. All ads are surreal in a sense: they connect disparate objects in strange formal systems, or place familiar objects in locations with which they have no obvious connection. We are so familiar with perfume bottles haunting desert islands and motor cars growing in fields of buttercups that their surreal qualities go unremarked. (Dali's 'Apparition of a Face and Fruit Dish on a Beach' could be the description of an everyday advertisement). What the B&H ads do, obliquely, is *refer* to surrealism as an 'Art' structure, and more particularly, they draw on the crux of surrealism – the assumption of an underlying sense. In the original Surrealist paintings, this sense was a psychoanalytic one, the logic of a dream. The fact that it wasn't immediately apparent guaranteed the depth of its existence.

B&H ads like the Mousetrap, the Birdcage, the Christmas Tree (and more recently, the Winston ads) make a formal play on doing exactly what all ads do: re-place a product in a context with which it has no 'natural' connection, so that it takes on meaning from its surroundings. The difference is that the B&H ads don't seek to naturalize this re-location, they play on its strangeness. The product doesn't come to mean 'parrot' or 'electric plug'. It is the context of 'Art' in which the product is being inserted.

And in this context, it is the very difficulty in understanding the images, and the absence of obvious connections, which indicates the genuinely 'cultured' status of the ads, and therefore, of the product. The ads are visual puzzles, they imply meanings one doesn't have access to. This suggests 'High Art' and thereby, exclusivity. A product for the discerning, the tasteful, the few. The legal restrictions on linking tobacco with social success are brilliantly by-passed. A B&H ad doesn't *depict* a social class (as, for example, Martini ads do) but implicitly, and flatteringly, *addresses* one, through its reference to Art and the assumed response. (Similarly, Players No. 6 have managed to imply exactly the social class of consumer they used to depict, in their imitation series which is much less 'difficult': while referring to the Benson and Hedges campaign, their 'down-market' version is reassuring, for people who didn't feel they 'got' the smarter images.)

In terms of class and taste, the Three Ducks ad is the most revealing. Flying ducks are tacitly a joke about 'bad' taste among those who assume theirs is 'good'. Just as the formal

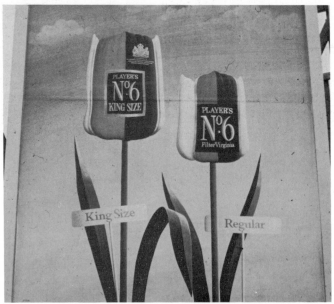

70

Naughty. But nice.

72

peculiarity of the picture is unsettling, with its distorted angles, stark primary colours and lack of realism, so the cosy lower-classness of the whole lifestyle implied by the ducks, is both scorned and threatened by the social snobbery (wrapped in a visual snobbery) of the image. This ad confirms the connection between Artistic and social values which underpins the whole series.

Quite the opposite effect is produced by the 'Mona Lisa' ad. This is a familiar reference, a picture that even the 'uneducated' have heard of. But more than that: here again, the connotations derived from its use of the 'Art' image exactly fit the overall social tone of the ad. The Mona Lisa's smile is a well-known mystique, famous, like Art, for its incomprehensibility. But here we have a perfectly ordinary, homey explanation! She is thinking of a real dairy cream cake. The inscrutable is suddenly brought into terms of everyday life, and, although this is clearly a joke, it is one with very deep-lying implications, about Art, inferiority, and the *relief* at being able to joke about something one feels is alien. And this relief is exactly like the pleasure of letting oneself go, and having a nice (but naughty) éclair. In relation to High Culture and Art, this ad is as reassuring as a cream cake. Even the caption recognizes both the transgression of tampering with 'Art' (naughty) and, simultaneously, the comforting sense such transgression brings (nice). This ad draws on exactly the same assumptions about 'Art' as the B&H ones, but invites the response of a different social group (and in particular, women).

The 'Picasseau' ad, like the 'Mona Lisa' ad, jokes about a well-known style with a familiarity that at once disarms and impresses: it successfully combines both ends of the spectrum. Even people who have never heard of cubism have heard of Picasso and know he often painted in strange square shapes, making the familiar (a woman, a guitar) alien. Here it's done so simply that anyone can 'get' it: the alien is re-familiarized. Yet it's done so stylishly that it also

reads like an in-joke for the arty. Anyone can grasp the visual joke – even the bubbles are square. Cleverly, this ad provides multiple values: snobbery, or reassurance. It depends how much you know about Art . . .

(City Limits, 1984)

ROYALTY AND REPRESENTATION

The key to the great significance and popularity of Royalty is that they are at once like us, and not like us. The institution of the family provides the central structure of identification which allows us to feel they are like us: after all, Royals marry, have children, worry about their teenage sons' affairs, love their gran, and so on, as the popular press constantly reports. On the other hand, they are quite obviously different from us: they are rich and famous – they are Royal, the rulers of the nation. However, the point about the royal family is that, unlike any other category of people who are rich and famous, they haven't *done* anything to be different (except be born) – they just *are*. In this sense, they are actually *not* special: they are not particularly clever, or particularly successful at anything, they do not have to be wildly attractive or strikingly original. No other group of people so consistently in the public eye, is so very *ordinary*. Boy George or Arthur Scargill are famous because of their *actions;* they have made choices: no member of the royal family has so existential a claim to fame. If they were not Royal, there would be nothing special about them at all. Seen from this angle, it becomes clear that the 'ordinariness' of the royal family is not just some ideological gag dreamed up by the media to befuddle the 'real' ordinary people:

inasfar as their personal attributes are concerned it is quite patently true. They are exactly no better and no worse than we are.

Because their only difference from us is precisely that they *are* Royal, the royal family has a quite unique role in social representation: they are ourselves writ large, they are the ordinary held up for everyone to see. In this sense one can talk about the royal family *as* representation before even moving on to the question of how *they* are represented (i.e. in imagery etc). The combination of similarity-but-difference (or association-but-difference) is the basic means of any representation[1]: for a picture of a tree to mean a tree it can't *be* a tree, but it does have to look like one. The image (or sign) must be similar to (or associated with) whatever it represents, without actually being it, or it couldn't stand *for* it. This idea of 'standing in' for something else[2] provides a useful way of linking the representation that we understand as a process of meaning, with the kind of representation that we connect with, say, Members of Parliament, who stand *for* us (supposedly) in parliament. This double sense of representation has implications in every area of social life. But its relevance to Royalty is that despite their position at the very top of the social pyramid, or rather, because of it, the royal family *stand for,* or represent, the broadest part of it, the popular, the masses of people who are not 'special' in any way. The American notion that anyone can become President means that their head of State not only stands for but also *shows* what the 'average person' can achieve. The President therefore functions as an *indexical* sign, a measure of something.[3] However, the royal family are neither elected nor replaceable, nor could 'we' ever be 'them': they represent us by sheer *analogy,* an *iconic* sign, to pursue Peirce's categories.[4] This way in which the royal family *parallels* our own, but at a distance, is the heart of its representative function. The Queen is a much loved popular figure who, far from being identified with the upper

classes, of which she might be seen as the very upmost, is strongly identified in people's minds with the ordinary population, the average kind of person. Not to recognize this, but to see the royal family as merely standing for privilege and wealth, is completely to misunderstand its place in people's hearts and minds, and its link, through the means of social representation described above, with 'the masses'.

Besides representing 'the people' by analogy, Royalty also embodies a strong principle of 'noblesse oblige', the notion of duty *to* 'the people'. It is felt that the Queen *cares*: nobody knows what she *thinks* about any political issue but she is allowed to express her 'concern', as palace press releases announced rather ambiguously over the miners' strike. The fact that striking miners' wives brought a petition to Buckingham Palace seeking support for their cause shows that it is by no means an entirely middle class or right-wing section of the population who believe that the Queen has their interests at heart. Prince Charles makes frequent public statements of concern over social issues, and, interestingly, sees his role as precisely that of a representative of public opinion, speaking for the 'ordinary person' who, not being Royal, is not so likely to be listened to. When interviewed after his controversial speech attacking architects for ignoring 'ordinary people's' tastes and wishes, Prince Charles explained that he felt many people would have liked to say the same thing but wouldn't have the chance, and he was expressing it largely on their behalf.[5] Perhaps the most extreme combination of all in this linking of Royalty with the 'masses' is the image of Princess Anne among starving children in Africa, or on one of many similar visits for the 'Save the Children Fund'. Royalty can be used to siphon off the conscience of a government or society; Princess Anne is hardly to blame personally for the deprivation of the Third World, yet something is deeply disturbing about this image of privilege showing concern for the poverty on which, in part at least, its wealth has been founded. It is as if the sense of a 'caring' society, once supposed to be enshrined in the Welfare State, has been displaced (who today thinks of the *state* as 'caring'?) onto the heads of State, Prince, Princess, Queen, who in reality can do little about anything. However, most people still feel that they are on 'our' side.

This kind of populism, in which the lowest classes of society can identify (at a distance) with the very top, is not the product of a *capitalist* class based society but, like the family itself, is a relic from an earlier, feudal order. Within the feudal system the family was not just a social unit, but the pattern for the whole social structure: a paternalistic hierarchy in which places were not achieved by effort, but given and fixed by God, the ultimate father of all: 'The rich man at his castle, the poor man at his gate, He made them high or lowly and ordered their estate'[6]. Although obviously class positions in modern society are still determined by birth, this *acceptance* of a social place determined by birth alone now seems to 'stick' only with Royalty, who are 'forgiven' for their position in a way that no other leading figures are. After all, it is merely an accident of birth that has made Prince Charles and not my brother the heir to the throne, whereas politicians, for example, are often felt to have 'pushed' their way to the top. Royalty can't, like the politician or industrialist, be blamed for their role in society; and our acceptance of *their* place tends to carry with it an acceptance of our own. The ideologies underlying this acceptance predate the bourgeois-protestant ethic in which people rise or fall by their own merits and labours, and, as I have suggested, incorporate something of the pre-capitalist order.

The effect of this, ideologically, is to by-pass the relations of modern capitalism while profoundly benefiting them. A stability based on a semi-feudal *loyalty* can conveniently underpin what is, of course, today a system of capitalist social relations – a system which is inherently unstable based as it is on competition and expansionism. In this context not only does the royal family provide a link with the past and a way of binding the nation into one big family ('The Granny of us all'), but in the midst of a 'liberal democracy' where the official political ideology is that of 'informed choice', it offers an anachronistic and quite unique form of populism incorporating both affection (based on identification) and obedience (based on difference). It paradoxically elevates the ordinary, while maintaining hierarchy and privilege.

This combination of the ordinary and the special represented *by* Royalty is manifested in the representation *of* Royalty through two basic modes: the informal and the formal. There is the intimate and casual private moment on the one hand; the spectacle of State occasions, the glamour of wealth and national tradition on the other. In one form of imagery the Royals are just like ourselves, in the other they are delightfully different. To see either one of these alone as the crucial representation of the royal family would be a mistake; it is the combination of the two which makes each so powerful. The formal, official aspect of Royalty is seen not only in the more 'regal' portraits and photographs of ceremonial events, but in the hundreds of commemorative medallions, mugs, crests, posters etc which are in many ways the modern form of pageantry. Formal 'Royal' occasions such as coronations and weddings give rise to a coinage of heraldic household articles whose charm lies in their combination of the important and the everyday. Conversely, the informal imagery of Royalty takes its interest from the fact that it *is* 'Royals' who are shown in otherwise completely unremarkable situations – walking a dog, holding a child, being pregnant. The enormous effort the *Sun* photographers took to sneak photographs of Princess Diana bathing when pregnant on holiday is striking for the very banality of the product: the whole point was to get shockingly *ordinary* pictures, far from glamorous, of a

An open letter to Prince William

FROM Marje

The Granny of us all

Dear Prince William

WHEN I heard that you were making your first public appearance on your Great-Grandma's eighty-second birthday, I couldn't help wondering if this was really the best kind of star-billing —for either of you.

Who, I mused, will steal the thunder? No doubt you'll make more noise than she will. Most babies, even well-behaved Royal ones, yell their heads off during their christening.

Your Great-Grandma will simply coo and murmur softly as she gazes proudly at the newest baby member of the great Royal clan.

One thing I am sure about: She'll be delighted to share the spotlight with you on this great day in both your lives.

As for you, well, it will all go right over your fluffy blond head.

You'll be as oblivious as any six-week-old boy to the pomp of the ceremony which will surround you.

You will have to wait until you're a bit older to discover what happened. Maybe in three or four years' time, your Mamma will show you the pictures taken at your christening and read all the bits out of the paper she'll have kept.

Gracious

She'll tell you, what a super baby you were and how well you behaved, considering you weren't old enough to understand Royal dignity and discipline and the imperative need to keep a stiff upper lip on all occasions like your Dad does.

Your Great - Grandmother naturally behaves at all times with the utmost composure and gracious charm behind which there's always a touch of merry mischief.

When you get old enough to appreciate her, oh boy, will you have a great buddy and ally on your side !

She is pretty about all her grandchildren and great-grandchildren. In fact, the entire British nation regard her as their grannie, too.

You're going to have to share her with about 50 million other people, plus several more millions dotted around the globe. Even lots of non-Britishers seem to have adopted her as their gran as well.

It isn't the least bit surprising. You will discover that she embodies all the qualities that make certain grandmothers so special.

She is warm and cuddly and loving and cheerful and as game as they come.

You'll never hear her moaning, even if her back's aching or her feet are killing her, or

> **She is cuddly, loving and as game as they come**

her face is positively aching with keeping her famous smile alight.

She knows what's expected of someone the people adore and she gives it to them. Wholeheartedly.

The way she'll give her love and attention to you.

You'll have a bit of competition, though, young William. There are your cousins Peter and Zara, for instance. She's the sort of grannie who will be very careful not to show favouritism. But it wouldn't surprise me if deep down, she had a particularly soft spot for you.

She's got one for your father. It's said he's her favourite among the grandchildren, though you can be sure she's never let the others feel any less loved.

And even if she does slip you an extra fiver or a few more smarties than she gives to your auntie Anne's children, she'll do it in such a subtle way that

they won't feel jealous or deprived.

She's got such a lot of love to give, has your Great-Grannie and I hope she'll go on to an even greater old age so that as a toddler and growing lad, you will be able to realise how great she really is.

You will discover that little children and their grannies have a very special understanding.

Somehow, however good and loving parents are children on the whole can't be friends with their Mums and Dads. They can love and respect them, obey them (or if they're naughty, disobey them), but being best

friends with them doesn't seem to quite work.

But a boy can be best friends with his grandmother. In your case, you are exceptionally fortunate to have a Grandmother and a Great-grannie.

Majestic

Your Grandmother is grand in every sense of the word, being the Queen and majestic and very busy with all her official engagements.

She will certainly find time for you and her other grandchildren but it's a bit hard for her as she works so hard.

Your Great-grandma works too, even at the age of 82 but she'll have more time to be your best friend.

She'll cuddle you if you feel blue, spoil you when no-one's looking and enrich your life, little William.

Cherish her and love her the way she deserves to be loved. You won't go far wrong with a Great-grandma like her as an example.

All the best to you and many happy returns to that wonderful lady.

Respectfully yours,

Marje Proops

CHILDREN'S FAVOURITE: The Queen Mother with a soldier's son in West Germany.

DAILY **Mirror**

Saturday, March 10, 1984   17p

Diana you MUSTN'T bite your nails!

By JAMES WHITAKER
and SHEREE DODD

PRINCESS Diana was told yesterday: "You mustn't bite your nails."

The playful telling off came from 81-year-old Mrs Winifred Beard.

Mrs Beard, a patient at the Sue Ryder home near Cheltenham, had just had a manicure when the Princess visited the home.

Di put on a mock stern manner and said: "You mustn't bite your nails, you know."

When Mrs Beard replied: "And you mustn't bite yours," Diana pulled a face and hid her hands behind her back.

Laugh

Mrs Beard said: "We all had a bit of a laugh."

An aide said that Diana did bite her nails until two years ago.

Diana told another patient that Charles does the washing-up at home. "Men can cope if they want," she said.

But while Di was looking good in a lilac coat and hat yesterday, her husband was stunning historic Moreton-in-Marsh, Gloucs., with an equally historic suit. It had four-inch wide lapels, creases, wrinkles . . . and even good old-fashioned turn-ups.

As he made his visit, local jokers were asking which came first — the town or the suit?

Charles, when DID you get that suit?

woman looking exactly like any other pregnant mum. There is as avid a drive to provide pictures of the Royals looking totally un-royal as there is to provide formal portraits of them – or more so. Yet the *Royalty* is always what gives the picture its value.

The captions accompanying such pictures in the popular press often furnish the key to this obsession: the Royals are spoken to as familiarly as if they were our next-door neighbours. Randy Andy is told not to be such a worry to his mum; Diana is told off for biting her nails; and so on. The occasion of Prince Henry's birth recently provided the opportunity for a little homily on sibling rivalry from Marje Proops in the *Mirror:* Prince William's mum and dad must try to make sure he doesn't feel too jealous of his new brother. In a certain sense, the public can actually be made to feel slightly superior to the royal family, since Royals' actions are available for comment and criticism (does Princess Margaret smoke too much? etc) in a way that no ordinary person's behaviour is. The urge to find embarassingly homely pictures of Royals is in part a wish to bring them down, to show that they are not really superior to us at all.

All this adds up to a function which, as I have suggested, is representative more of a *norm,* a way of 'average' family life and leisure, than of something totally upper class and distant. The royal family may technically be the most 'upper class' in the country, but the life-style they represent is very lower-to-middle middle class – never arty or highbrow (Prince Charles was violently attacked for 'middlebrow taste' after his architecture speech) and with no intellectual pretensions or extreme glamour. The Queen was recently criticized for looking 'dowdy' and wearing old-fashioned clothes on a visit to Canada. But it is precisely this which makes her image what it is.[7] Princess Diana may provide some fairy-tale recession glamour in her ball gowns and wedding dress, but average royal family appearance

('Charles, when DID you get that suit?') is far from jet-setting or stylish. Their image when 'at home' is very much a cosy fireside one – you could imagine them listening to Radio Four but not so easily reading *Finnegan's Wake.* The middle-of-the-road nature of their cultural image is crucial to the modern function of Royalty. It was Queen Victoria who first projected such an image – her and Albert's family were the epitome of middle-class (Victorian) domestic culture, and during her reign photography began to play a formative role in the representation of that culture. Today, shots of the royal family in their living room round the fireplace, or having a picnic with their dogs, are some of the most-used images in 'royal albums' and magazines. And everything about such photos seems to invoke, not so much aristocratic values, as the values of the traditional upper-working class/lower-middle class family.

There are two key points about this phenomenon. One is that the royal family suggests nationhood through *home* values as much as through the more blatantly nationalistic values of war etc. Much was made in the popular press of the fact that Prince Andrew served in the Falklands War 'like any other boy': his mum was worried sick and hoped he would do his best but couldn't wait to see him safely home. It is another of the contradictions in the royal family's image that although they occupy the very highest places in the armed forces (the Queen is ultimately Commander-in-Chief of all of them) their service (as when Prince Charles did his naval training) is seen as egalitarian – they have to muck in with everyone else. In an album of the Queen Mother we are told that during World War 2 'Princess Elizabeth persuaded her parents to let her take part in national service like other girls of her age.' A kind of nationalism through populism is evident in quotes like this: the real point of the sentence isn't that the Princess did 'national service' but that she did it '*like other girls her age*'. And the subtext is that she had a relationship with her parents like that of any girl her age – a

1942; The Royal Family at home in Buckingham Palace, the present Queen, then a girl, knitting a sock for the war effort.

A recent domestic scene of the Queen and Prince Philip.

picture of a normal family is subtly conveyed. It is in this picture of family values that the values of 'nation' are enshrined.

The second point concerns class. The royal family *are* aristocratic, they engage in upper-class activities like hunting and shooting, they live on vast estates. Yet, as I have tried to show, they have in some ways a very solid lower-middle class image. Post-Victorian royalty seems to have combined both the structure of a feudal aristocracy and the culture of the capitalist bourgeois and petit-bourgeois, incorporating the most conservative elements of both systems. Moreover, the fact that the structure itself belongs to an earlier system, historically, keeps those at the bottom of the present social structure in a state of emotional feudalism, looking backwards instead of round about. It is, however, the petit-bourgeois – the class with the least clear place under capitalism – that this opportunity for looking backwards really appeals to, and for whom the royal family is an especially important focus.

The importance of a class analysis in understanding royalty and its representation is shown in the fact that it is exactly the kind of populist loyalty felt for the royal family that Mrs Thatcher is trying to harness to her own support. Putting it very crudely, if the Queen combines petit-bourgeois culture with a benign feudalism, Margaret Thatcher is aiming to combine petit-bourgeois culture with a ruthless capitalism. It is reported that the Queen does not get on with Mrs Thatcher and sees the Prime Minister as trying to encroach on her prerogative and territory. A clear example of this was the 'Falklands Victory Parade' when Margaret Thatcher presided over the trooping of Falklands soldiers in the way the Queen usually does – the Queen herself was not present. Thus Mrs Thatcher seems to have identified herself with the cause of 'The Nation' more than the Queen. This is in itself interesting, but there was further reported friction over the Queen's rejection of the govern-

Not a Royal Procession, but Mrs. Thatcher's Falklands Victory Parade.

During a visit to Canada Prince Charles is made an Honorary Indian of the Kanai Tribe.

ment's recommendation not to visit certain Commonwealth countries at a time of disturbance. The Queen and the royal family have a strong identification with the Commonwealth – a force now virtually defunct, politically of little interest to the government. The Royal relation to Commonwealth is, of course, part of the colonialist legacy and is in no way progressive, despite being pictured as benevolent. Yet it is a measure of the times that the Queen appears to have more relation to Commonwealth citizens than the government, with its explicitly racist immigration policies and Mrs Thatcher's infamous 'alien cultures' (we are being swamped by) speech. It is hard to imagine Mrs Thatcher cavorting with black tribal leaders and joining in 'alien' ceremonies in the way that the royal family are so frequently (albeit patronizingly) shown doing.

None of this is to suggest for a moment that the royal family are a progressive force. It is simply that the government of the day have introduced what one might call a new hardness to the political scene, and in this climate the royal family appears as almost liberal. This is not for any personal reasons so much as for the reason that, as an institution, it refers back to a fundamentally non-capitalist scheme of things (like so many car ads, beer ads etc) and a different set of values. In a peculiar way these are closer to the popular ideology of the 'People's War' and the Welfare State of the '40s and '50s, which also embodies the idea of 'caring from above' (though in quite a different form) than they are to contemporary capitalist ideology. The benign consensus which the Queen seems to represent politically no longer exists. In both its ancient feudal structure and its modern 'benevolent' ideology, Royalty belongs to another world. This provides at once an escape from our present way of life, and a justification for it: the human face of hereditary rule at a time when the elected government is increasingly *in*human.

(*Ten-8*, 1985)

NOTES

1. *Similarity* with its referent (the thing referred to) is the means of most pictorial representation, while verbal representation, i.e. language, works by the *association* of a word with its referent, i.e. the sound or look of the word 'tree' is associated with the object tree in English. (See Saussure, *Course in General Linguistics* Ch. 1).

2. C. S. Peirce defined a sign as 'something which stands to somebody for something else in some respect or capacity'. *(Collected Papers)*

3. Peirce further distinguished between three kinds of sign; the best explanation of his definitions is found in Peter Wollen's *Signs and Meaning in the Cinema* pp. 122–3: 'An index is a sign by virtue of an existential bond between itself and its object' – in the sense that smoke is a sign of fire, or a footprint indicates a foot. The sign is in each case an *effect* of the thing it stands for, it has a relation to it in the material world.

4. An icon, according to Peirce, is a sign which represents its object mainly by its similarity to it . . . thus, for instance, the portrait of a man resembles him.' (Wollen). The third kind of sign described by Peirce is the symbol, which he defines as having an arbitrary relation to what it represents. Almost all words come into this category, or any arbitrary system like, for example, Morse code.

5. See interview in the *Daily Mirror, 5/6/84.*

6. From the hymn 'All Things Bright and Beautiful'.

7. The Queen is not required to be a flamboyant first lady in the style of Jackie Kennedy or Nancy Reagan; she doesn't need to. The point about the British class system is that the higher up you are, the less you are supposed to 'try'. It is important to realize that despite all the public attention focused on Princess Diana and her appearance, the obsession with her wardrobe, hairstyle and so on is only possible because the fundamental 'values' of Royalty are firmly anchored in the Queen, and therefore the frivolity can go elsewhere.

A PIECE OF THE ACTION

Images of 'Woman' in the
Photography of Cindy Sherman

When I rummage through my wardrobe in the morning I am not merely faced with a choice what to wear. I am faced with a choice of images: the difference between a smart suit and a pair of overalls, a leather skirt and a cotton dress, is not just one of fabric and style, but one of identity. You know perfectly well that you will be seen differently for the whole day, depending on what you put on; you will appear as a particular kind of woman with one particular identity *which excludes others*. The black leather skirt rather rules out girlish innocence, oily overalls tend to exclude sophistication, ditto smart suit and radical feminism. Often I have wished I could put them all on together, or appear simultaneously in every possible outfit, just to say, How dare you think any one of these is *me*. But also, See, I can be all of them.

This seems to me exactly what Cindy Sherman achieves in her series of 'Film Stills' and later 'Untitled' photographs. To present all those surfaces at once is such a superb way of flashing the images of 'Woman' back where they belong, in the recognition of the beholder. Sherman's pictures force upon the viewer that elision of image and identity which women experience all the time: as if the sexy black dress made you *be* a femme fatale, whereas 'femme fatale' is, precisely, an image, it needs a viewer to function at all. It's also just one splinter of the mirror, broken off from, for example, 'nice girl' or 'mother'. Sherman stretches this phenomenon in two directions at once – which makes the tension and sharpness of her work. *Within* each image, far from deconstructing the elision of image and identity, she very smartly leads the viewer to *construct* it; but by presenting a whole lexicon of feminine identities, all of them played by 'her', she undermines your little constructions as fast as you can build them up.

'Image' has a double sense, both as the kind of woman fantasized (is your 'image' aggressive, cute, femme fatale, dumb blonde etc), and as the actual representation, the photograph. What Sherman does is to make you see type of 'woman', of femininity, as inseparable from the literal presentation of the image – lighting, contrast, composition, photographic style. The 'Film Stills' are the most obvious example of this. The grainy print and ominous shadows in *Untitled Film Still # 4* are part of what makes up our idea of the woman shown leaning against the door. The low angle, crisp focus and sharp contrasts of *Untitled Film Still # 16* are part of the woman's sophisticated yet fragile image, just as the slightly soft focus and low contrast of *# 40* are part of *her* more pastoral, Renoir-esque femininity. The composition of the recognizably 'New Wave Art Movie' Still *# 63,* the smallness of the figure in the harshly geometric architecture, is part of the little-girl-lostness that we feel as coming from the woman. In the Untitled Film Stills we are constantly forced to recognize a visual style (often you could name the director) simultaneously with a type of femininity. The two cannot be pulled apart. The image suggests that there is a particular kind of femininity in the *woman* we see, whereas in fact the femininity is in the image itself, it *is* the image – 'a surface which suggests nothing but itself, and yet in so far as it suggests there is something behind it, prevents us from considering it as a surface'.[1]

Untitled Film Still # 40

Untitled Film Still # 4

Untitled Film Still # 63

Untitled # 80

94

Apart from the interest of this for anyone analyzing how film and photographic representations work, it is, as I have tried to suggest, particularly important for women. I find the recognition of this process, that the 'woman' is constructed in the image, very liberating; I want to say 'You see?!' to any man standing next to me looking at the photos in the exhibition. Because the viewer is forced into complicity with the way these 'women' are constructed: you recognize the styles, the 'films', the 'stars', and at that moment when you recognize the picture, your reading *is* the picture. In a way, 'it' is innocent: *you* are guilty, you supply the femininity simply through social and cultural knowledge. As one reviewer says, 'she shows us that, in a sense, we've bought the goods.'[2] The stereotypes and assumptions necessary to 'get' each picture are found in our own heads. Yet, at the risk of being attacked as 'essentialist', I really do think the complicity of viewing is different for women and men. For women, I feel it shows us that we needn't buy the goods, or at least, we needn't buy them as being our 'true selves'. But in a discussion at the first Sherman retrospective in Britain, I remember a man getting incredibly worked up about how sexist the images were, and furious at 'Cindy Sherman'. He kept saying there were enough images of women as sexual objects, passive, doll-like, all tarted up. Although his rhetoric sounded Right On, I was certain his anger must have come from a sense of his own involvement, the way those images speak not only *to* him but *from* him – and he kept blaming Sherman herself for it, deflecting his sexism onto her, as if she really was a bit of a whore. This idea of what she 'really is' I'll return to later. But the way we are forced to supply the femininity 'behind' the photos through recognition is part of their power in showing how an ideology works – not by undoing it, but by *doing* it. The moment we recognize a 'character', it is as if she must already exist.

For what we construct from the surface of each picture is

an interior, a mixture of emotions. Each setting, pose and facial expression seems literally to express an almost immeasurable interior which is at once mysteriously deep, and totally impenetrable: a feminine identity. Obviously this is what acting is about, but these still images are like frozen moments of performance and so the sense of personality seems more trapped in the image itself. It is both so flat, and so full (it seems) of feeling. But what links the emotions portrayed in the pictures is that they are all emotional *responses*. The woman's expression is like an imprint of a situation, there is some action and her face registers a *re*action. Certain photos make this very explicit: *Untitled # 96,* where a girl holds a scrap of newspaper in her hand, shows precisely the way that we read into her fundamentally 'unreadable' face some emotional response which is both very definite, and entirely ambiguous. She looks thoughtful, but whether she is happy or unhappy, worried or perfectly all right, we have no clue. She looks, exactly, uncertain. Yet between the newspaper cutting and her face there is an endless production of significance which seems inevitable (it's always already started) and almost clear in its vagueness. Another photo from the same group, *Untitled # 90,* shows a teenager lying, equally ambiguous in her expression, by a telephone. Is she happily dreaming, or anxiously awaiting a call? (It's just like the ads for home pregnancy testing kits which manage to get the model looking both as if she's hopefully waiting for the good news of having a baby, *and* as if she can't wait to be put out of her fear that she might be pregnant.) Either way, her expression is an index of something or someone else, something we don't know about but which everything in the frame points to. (In semiotic terms it literally is an index, as a footprint is to a foot – a relevant metaphor since so many Sherman women look as if they were trodden on by men, fate, or a B-movie plot.) With the cutting, the telephone, or the letter in *Untitled Film Still # 5* (where there seems to be a response to

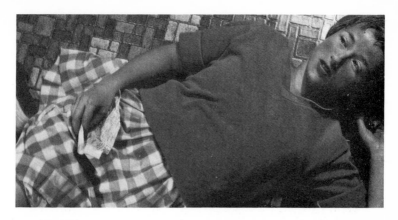

Untitled # 96

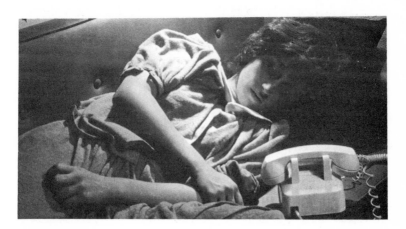

Untitled # 90

Untitled Film Still # 21

Untitled Film Still # 5

two things – the letter, and someone else off screen left) something is put in the image as a snippet representative of the unknown narrative; but these images simply make explicit what happens in all of them, which is that meaning is thrown endlessly back and forth between a 'woman' and a story. The cutting gives expression to the face, the face gives a story to the cutting.

This is exactly what happens in films, newsphotos, adverts and media generally. An image of a woman's face in tears will be used by a paper or magazine to show by *impression* the tragedy of a war, or the intensity of, say, a wedding. From the face we are supposed to read the emotion of the event. But conversely, it is the event that gives the emotion to the face; we have to know whether it is a war or a wedding to interpret correctly its well of meaning. Similarly in films the use of close-ups – woman screaming, woman weeping, woman watching, woman terrified, woman impressed – function as an imprint of the action, like a thermometer constantly held to the narrative. And no matter what the nature or content of the imprint, it is this imprintedness itself which seems to constitute femininity.

In Sherman's 'Film Stills' the very reference to film invites this interpretation. Film stills are by definition a moment in a narrative. In every still, the woman suggests something other than herself, she is never complete: a narrative has to be invoked. Who, or what, is the dark-haired woman in *# 16* responding to? What is troubling the Hitchcockian heroine in *# 21*? What is that young French girl in *# 40* looking sideways at? But in the later works simply called 'Untitled', the questions are perhaps more interesting and subtle, precisely because they aren't presented as 'film stills'. *Something* is worrying, not to say frightening, the women in photos like *Untitled # 80* – at least 90 minutes' worth of something. In this group, back-projection is used to create the setting, the backdrop scenario which interacts with the woman's face to produce the story, and the visual effect

Untitled Film Still # 16

stays quite close to film. The next series, from which *Untitled # 90* and *# 96* were selected, comes closer in to the woman's body than many of the earlier works, but still adds a prop, a clue to the story. However, the most recent work uses no props and a less 'filmy' style, so we seem to be nearer an actual woman, presented more 'neutrally'. These photos are closer to adverts than films; they still rely on clothes, lighting and a facial expression which is evocative of something outside the frame. Here we don't get *any* of the story, only the response.

But the point is, the story *is her*. As we piece together, or guess, or assume, some meaning in the narrative, we find that the meaning is the woman. She appears to express the meaning of events. How like every narrative and photographic medium this is, and also how like actual life, the 'they've got it, she wears it' of personal relations. In tapping the relation between women and meaningfulness Sherman's work resonates through many other areas. Certainly it also illuminates the process of reading all still images, especially adverts, in the way objects, details, arrangements and settings construct a story and an identity simultaneously. Women are not always necessarily a part of this visual and ideological process. But in Sherman's work, what comes out of the imagined narratives is, specifically, femininity. It is not just a range of feminine expressions that are shown but the *process* of the 'feminine' as an effect, something acted on.

However, this femininity is not all form and no content. The emotions that bounce between the narrative and the woman in each picture, though unclear, are nearly all suggestive of fear, suspicion, vulnerability, anxiety, or at best uncertainty. And Sherman brilliantly shows how this vulnerability is linked with eroticism, not always through explicitly 'sexual' poses – as in *Untitled # 103* and some of the earlier much publicized Film Stills (not shown here) – but through performing femininity at their intersection. In the earlier work, particularly, there always seems to be a sense of menace, the woman is under threat. And her vulnerability is always erotic, rather in the way that many horror movies which involve no explicit sex at all give an erotic spin-off just through having a terrified woman constantly in vulnerable positions. So strongly is femininity evoked in these situations that they have to be *sexual* – is there any definition of femininity that isn't? That's why, in so many of Sherman's images, simply the distress or passivity of the women figures feels faintly pornographic – I say that to be descriptive rather than pejorative. I feel Sherman simply brings to the surface very clearly that same whiff of the pornographic that I personally feel about so many of Hitchcock's heroines, frightened, blonde and vulnerable, or Godard's use of Anna Karina and other women stars as fathomless icons of femininity, passive repositories of desire. Sherman's women with their parted lips and their stories in their eyes (very Bob Dylan) are something to get off on in their very uncertainty. And in linking the erotic and the vulnerable she has hit a raw nerve of 'femininity'. I don't by this mean women (though we do experience it) but the *image* of Woman, an imaginary, fragmentary identity found not only in photos and films but in the social fabric of our thoughts and feelings.

It is so important to stress the difference not because 'femininity' is a bad, false, two-dimensional construct that is forced upon us (even if it feels that way) but precisely because, ultimately, it isn't any one thing at all. It can only exist in opposition to something else, like one half of a see-saw. In Sherman's pictures, the way the woman is *affected by* something makes her like an *effect,* her face stamped by events, and I have tried to argue that this produces the feminine sexual identity which comes across. But what is crucial to the reading of Sherman's work is also the opposition between the images. 'Essentially feminine' as they all are, they are all different. This not only rules out the idea that any one of them *is* the 'essentially feminine', but also shows, since each *seems* to be it, that there can be no such thing. Yet so tenacious is the wish for this set of psychic garments to turn out to be actual skin, that almost every time Sherman's work is written about the issue of Cindy Sherman 'herself' comes into it. She has often been thought of as *indulging* in self-images, wishing secretly to be like Marilyn Monroe, posing as a sexy heroine. From the notion that her work springs from a desire to be more glamorous, follows the idea that she is not 'really' as attractive as her heroines, the glamour is not allowed to be hers.

The best example of such an approach is Waldemar Janusczak's review of her retrospective at Bristol in the *Guardian:* 'You see her as she sees herself, a small, scrawny girl from Buffalo, a mousey blond who dreams of becoming a peroxide starlet. Her wigs don't always fit and her bra has to be padded.' What a combination of put-down and turn-on! 'Behind the Marilyn Monroe character you finally find Cindy Sherman.' How? Does he know her? 'She is at her best looking intense, staring into the distance as intently as if it were her own past – which of course it is . . .' and finally, 'Several times she appears to be recoiling from the harsh stare of her own camera, like a scared animal trapped in a car's headlights. This too, you sense, is the real Cindy Sherman.'[3] This all reads like a patently sexual fantasy, as if she were at somebody's mercy (his). If she were a man he would not even continue using her first name as well as surname beyond the first paragraph; and this detail of language might make him have to treat her as an artist, in control of her work. As it was, even the image selected to illustrate the article was one of the most sexually provocative. I have quoted this review in detail first to show that it is a possible response to the work (basically for men) but second, because I think that this false search for the 'real' her is exactly what the work is about, and it leads people like Waldemar Janusczak right up the garden path. The attempt to find the 'real' Cindy Sherman is unfulfillable, just as it is for anyone, but what's so interesting is the obsessive *drive* to find that identity.

This comes out particularly in comments on the later photos. Almost every critic has felt the recent work is in some way moving closer to Sherman 'herself'. The catalogue introduction calls it 'free of references to archetypes' and says that 'dressed in today's clothes . . . the(se) portraits seem more refined, natural and closer to Cindy Sherman herself.'[4] But in the more recent photos there seem to me to be sets of contrasts that function in the same way as the earlier 'Film Stills', only even more pointedly. For some reason most critics have seen *Untitled # 103* but somehow gone blind to *Untitled # 104,* which immediately follows it and would stand beside it in a gallery. There, right next to the sexy Monroe-type image is a different one – not necessarily unsexy or unsexual but very boyish, much more alert, wearing an old teeshirt – and, most important, they are both her. The fact that it *is* Cindy Sherman performing each time is precisely what undermines the idea that any one image is 'her'. It reminds me of the Cachet ad: 'It won't be the same on any two women . . . the perfume as individual as *you* are.' This promise is followed by a bunch of images of different 'femininities', each of which is meant to be a different *woman* (using Cachet); whereas what Sherman shows is that anyone can 'be' all of them, and none.

In the recent photos the issue seems to be pushed still farther, beyond different femininities and across the border of femininity/masculinity. This is particularly powerful because the later images do appear more 'realistic', though of course they are nothing of the sort. *Untitled # 116* and *# 112* both seem very straightforward, 'natural' poses compared with the earlier set-ups. Both are 'dressed in today's clothes', yet it is the subtlety in the difference between the clothes that makes one image very feminine, the other masculine. In *# 116* the lighting, pose, expression, gaze, hair, skin, all spell femininity; subtly, but as clearly as in *Film Still # 40*. But *# 112* is sharper: the pointed collar, the shorts, the 'harder' gaze, less unfixed than the other, all produce a 'masculine' reading. The way the later images move towards, not simply sexual ambiguity (as if that were an identity) but a juxtaposing of 'feminine' and 'masculine' identities, seems to demolish once and for all the idea that either of these is something that can be fully inhabited (and also puts paid to the wet-dream of Sherman as frightened animal or girl in padded bra).

For the identities elusively suggested, and so obsessively sought, are trapped, not in a car's headlights (!) but, literally, in the light of the photographic print: the lighting which makes the image possible on that surface which is ultimately nothing more than a flattened reaction to light. In *Untitled # 110* no face is even visible in the darkness, all that the lighting lets us see is an arm, a sleeve, some soft fabric, glowing as golden as an advert. There is only just enough photographic information for us to recognize what the image is of at all, and here again we are forced to realize how these effects on their own (as in so many ads) conjure up a feminine presence. The viewer is pushed as far as possible, to search in shadows for what isn't there on the page, but which the few shapes of light suggest *is* there. Femininity is trapped in the image – but the viewer is snared too. A similar and very witty rebuffing of our 'reading in' is found in *Untitled Film Still # 46*, where all that's visible of the woman is a diving mask looking up from the sea. We can't even see the face, and barely the eyes, yet the joke is, it *still* seems full of meaning.

In images like this one, in the whole range of work, in the juxtapositions made, there seems to me an enormous amount of wit. The conflation of Cindy Sherman as the imagined character in her performance, and Sherman as the artist, always ends up with some idea of 'her' as her heroines, frightened, vulnerable, threatened and uncertain.

Untitled # 103

Untitled # 104

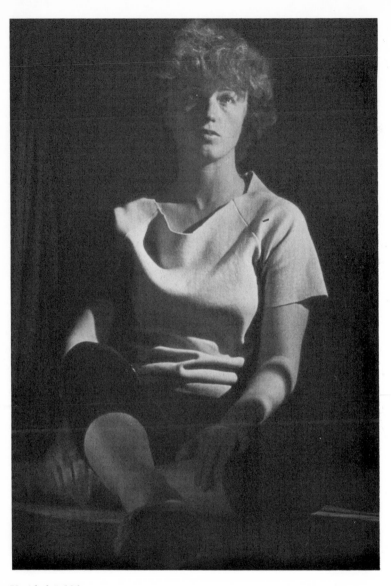

Untitled # 116

Untitled # 112

Untitled # 110

110

Untitled Film Still # 46

But clearly as an artist Sherman is sharp, controlled, intelligent, witty. Couldn't these qualities of the work itself, rather than being swamped by that femininity she exposes, reflect back on it as a biting comment? Obviously the dialectic between Sherman as performer and photographer is important; after all, she *does* choose to present *herself* (in disguise) in her pictures. The identities she acts out may be passive and fearful. But look what she *does* with them, what she *makes:* she is in control. In its very last line, the catalogue blurb turns on some of Sherman's critics: 'the women she represents, they say, are too artificial to be experienced as real people' and ends by asking poignantly, 'Is vulnerability as unreal as all that?'[5] Well, no, obviously not. But both the critics referred to, and the writer of the commentary, are opposing 'artificial' and 'real' in a way that has no meaning where femininity is concerned, which is why I started this piece with the wardrobe syndrome. Femininity is multiple, fractured, and yet each of its infinite surfaces gives the illusion of depth and wholeness. Realizing this means that we as women don't have to get trapped trying to 'be' the depth behind a *surface,* and men just might bang their heads up against it and stop believing in that reflected space. Sherman's work is more than either a witty parody of media images of women, or a series of self-portraits in a search for identity. The two are completely mixed up, as are the imagery and experience of femininity for all of us. Others might try to break open that web of mirrors, but Sherman's way of revealing it is just to keep on skilfully turning the kaleidoscope where a few fragments of fantasy go a long way.

(Screen, 1983)

NOTES

1. J. L. Baudry, 'The Mask' in 'Writing, Fiction Ideology' *Afterimage* (UK) Spring 1974

2. Michael Starenko, 'What's an Artist To Do?' *Afterimage* (US) Jan. 1983.

3. Waldemar Janusczak, 'Here's Looking at You, Kid' *Guardian* May 19, 1983

4. Els Barents, Introduction to *Cindy Sherman Catalogue.*

5. Ibid p.14.

FAMILY, EDUCATION, PHOTOGRAPHY

The crucial importance of the family as an institution in maintaining the State is agreed upon by radical feminists and government ministers alike. Official recognition of its role was revealed in the proposed 'Ministry of Marriage' some years back, but it has never been any secret that family life is the backbone of the nation. Its economic value to capitalism in providing both the unpaid maintenance of the labour force, and a floating pool of 'reserve labour', i.e. women, has been well documented in Marxist and feminist writings. It also plays a direct ideological role in maintaining the status quo, through channelling the socialization of children into the accepted social structure, a role it shares with 'education'. These functions of the family show that it is intimately connected with what Gramsci calls 'political society' or 'The State'.[1]

But what is contradictory about the *ideology* of the family is that it appears as the area of life most distant from the State, most 'private' and entirely non-political. While this is by no means a new phenomenon, it is worth noting that a major Tory achievement in the years leading up to and after 1979 has been to imbue the family with an aura of independence and individualism in total opposition to the State, and particularly the Welfare State: so that while drawing heavily on the economic and social support of the family the government can manage to suggest that this burden is a gift of freedom, a seal of separateness from itself. The representation of the family as an autonomous emotional unit cuts across class and power relations to imply that we all share the same experience. It provides a common sexual and economic goal: images of family life hold out pleasure and leisure as the fulfilment of desires which, if not thus contained, could cause social chaos.

These images almost invariably take the form of photographs, and have done since the middle of the 19th century. However, photography is not just the means *through* which ideological representations are produced; like the family, it is an economic institution with its own structures and ideology. It is possible to distinguish three different production relationships in the area of photography and the family:

1. *The photograph as commodity in the 'public' sphere:*

   A photographer produces a photograph which is a commodity bought by a magazine, newspaper or advertising agency. It is 'consumed' by us metaphorically, as viewers, but we do not actually buy the image on, for example, a billboard. Often the photographs which are the commodities of greatest value in this market are of families, e.g. the Royal family, Cecil Parkinson's family, Sting visiting wife and new baby in hospital, etc. In this sphere families can *look* at representations not of themselves, but of other families they are encouraged to identify with themselves.

2. *The photograph as commodity in the 'private' sphere:*

   A photographer produces (usually in a studio) a photograph which is a commodity bought by the person/people photographed, mainly families (or would-be families, like engaged couples). In this sphere individual families can *buy* representations of themselves.

3. *The camera as commodity in the 'private' sphere:*

When a photograph is taken by someone who is not a 'photographer' i.e. an amateur, usually in a family, the photograph itself is not a saleable commodity (unlesss it by chance shows something of public importance, or is a baby snap of a current pop-star etc). It is then the *camera* and *processing* which are the economic focus of the photographic industry; the value of photographs as commodities in the first two examples above, is preserved through the clear ideological instructions in camera/ processing advertisements about how and what to photo- graph. In this sphere families can *produce* representations of themselves.

I shall deal with the first category last, since public images of the family rely almost entirely on the styles and implications of the second two. Royal wedding photos differ only in scale from ordinary commissioned wedding photos (category 2); advertising images of happy families playing frisbee or eating picnics differ only in contrivance and technique from the arrangements of family leisure found in private albums (category 3). There is also another, somewhat different area – *Photography in 'Education':* where on the one hand photos *not* sold as commodities take on the function of recording and monitoring, and on the other, photos of school groups, teams, or individual children become commodities sold to parents and other family relations. In this sphere photogra- phy occupies a position somewhere between the family album and criminal surveillance.

Perhaps the most influential family image in our culture has been that of the Madonna and child; father was absent long before he had to hold the camera. However, as the image of the family unit became secularized during the Renaissance, it became traditional for wealthy families to record and display their spiritual and material bonds through oil paintings of the entire family group; surrounded by land, possessions and, perhaps in a corner, a few discreet symbols of the mortality against which those possessions were shored. Only the upper classes could afford to commission such self-imagery; certainly poorer families *were* painted, but not at their own request. They featured as subjects for the more democratically minded artists who would, in this case, keep their pictures, not sell them to their poverty-stricken sitters. (This tradition lingers on in documentary photography, where the poor, the foreign and the injured are still regarded as having no stake in the images they provide.)

This gap between those who could and could not afford to *own* pictures of themselves was dramatically narrowed by the advent of photographic portraiture in the mid-19th century. Early daguerreotypes had, like paintings, been unique and more expensive objects, but by the 1860s the possibility of photographic printing on paper brought this form of representation within the reach of the middle classes. Because at this stage photography was still a cumbersome affair, photographs were taken in the photographer's studio, which was furnished with a variety of props and backdrops, available equally to clients of all classes. It is sometimes quite difficult to tell the class of the stiffly posed Victorian couples leaning against classical pillars or standing in front of drapes, as they would be dressed in their best clothes and removed from their day-to-day surroundings.[2]

By the 1880s cameras were more mobile and could more easily enter the home space. Yet still the conventions of pose and setting were shared by working, middle and upper class alike. Queen Victoria was the first monarch to realize the marvellous ideological opportunities offered by photography and insisted on always being represented as a wife and mother, rather than a ruler. Photography played not merely an incidental but a central role in the development of the contemporary ideology of the family, in providing a form of representation which cut across classes, disguised social differences, and produced a sympathy of the exploited with their exploiters. It could make all families look more or less alike.

As the technology has become cheaper, the apparent democratization achieved in the *image* with Victorian photography, has now extended to the *means of production* of the image. Just as, in the last century, more people were able to own photographs, now more people are able to own cameras. Yet it is not entirely true to say that father (occasionally mother) has replaced the studio photographer. As cameras have become available on the mass market, the distinction between 'professional' and 'amateur' has been drawn more rigidly than ever before. Camera advertisements make quite clear that David Bailey or Don McCullin are allowed to take completely different kinds of pictures from us, even though the aspiring 'amateur' may use the same equipment (and make his wife look ten years younger). This demarcation is important, because with the slipping of the means of production into civilian hands, as it were, it becomes all the more important to control the kinds of images produced. This is achieved through convention, advertising, and even the images you find on the covers of the little folder your negatives are returned in from the labs. It is quite clear that the spoils of a holiday abroad are meant to be snaps of children on beaches, rather than shots of foreign political events.

Family photographs today divide into two different types: the formal, of weddings, christenings, graduation and so on, where professional photographers are still frequently used, and the informal, of holidays and other leisure time. The formal are a record, a kind of proof that the traditional landmarks of life have been reached, and these pictures have much in common with early 'posed' family photos. However, with the informal arrives a new element, never so highly developed as in contemporary family photography: the necessity of 'FUN'.

120

The Fairmont Family.
Of San Francisco, New Orleans and Dallas.

Memories are made of this.

121

In this modern 'democratic' idea, just as in the earlier levelling notion of the *dignity* of the family, photography plays a formative role.[3] The 'instant fun' offered by the Polaroid camera ad is both the fun *of* the picture, that process that takes place 'before your eyes', and the fun *in* the picture, smiles and jolly moments frozen into one of those objects which create the systematic misrepresentation of childhood and family life. But it is as if the guarantee 'before your eyes' ensured the very reality of the emotion pictured. The more transparent the process, the more indisputably real the content. And the dominant content, in home family photography, seems always to be pleasure. In earlier family images it seemed enough for the family members to be presented to the camera, to be *externally* documented; but now this is not enough, and *internal* states of constant delight are to be revealed on film. Fun must not only be had, it must be *seen* to have been had.

This raises the more psychoanalytic question of what is repressed in family photographs. Because besides being used externally as a unit of social cement, the family is also an extremely oppressive thing to be *in*. Photography erases this experience not only from the outside, in adverts of happy, product-consuming families, it also erases it from within, as photos of angry parents, crying children or divorced spouses are selected for non-appearance in the family album. It is of great significance within a family which photos are kept and which discarded, and also who takes photos of whom; and it is a fact not often thought worth commenting on that children are always the ones 'taken' (though older children may own cameras). In the Kodak ad 'Memories are made of this' it is father's hand that reaches for the camera in the foreground, to snap mother and the children who are unaware of his action. The ad stresses this with the barrier of the hedge, which makes father's photographic activity seem surreptitious, sneaky, almost voyeuristic.

But the important point is, *whose* memories are being made of this? It is by and large *parents'* memory that family photos represent, since parents took and selected the pictures. Yet children are offered a 'memory' of their own childhoods, made up of images constructed entirely by others. The hegemony of one class over another in representing public history, which offers us 'memories' of social life through TV and newsphotos, is paralleled in microcosm by this dominance of one version of family history, which represses much lived experience.

Yet as psychoanalysis has shown, nothing repressed ever disappears, and we may often be able to read in family photos 'clues' to their repressed elements. Walter Benjamin says that 'photography makes aware for the first time the optical unconscious, just as psychoanalysis discloses the instinctual unconscious'.[4] I would go further and say that the two are not only parallel; the 'optical unconscious' may on occasion reveal the 'instinctual unconscious'. I discovered a personal example of this on examining old photographs that

I found not in an album but loose in a drawer at my parents' house. To this day I have no memory of jealousy at my sister's birth when I was not yet two. Family mythology on the subject stated quite clearly that I had been a 'good, grown-up girl' and welcomed the new baby from the start; I must have cottoned on that this was expected as I can remember nothing else. Yet I was struck not only by the undeniably anxious and ambiguous looks that I gave the baby in all early pictures, but by the surprising fact that we were virtually the same size, and I had not been a grown-up girl at all.

Most 'education' goes hand in hand with families in repressing children and guiding them towards their niche in society; school and college photos reflect this with their family-like groupings. The school photo with the head in the centre, staff clustered around, juniors cross-legged on the ground, prefects at the back, looks like the portrait of an extended Victorian dynasty. (Of course, the traditional way to defy the convention of the slowly-panning school photograph was to run around the back and appear twice.) However, most schools today have replaced or supplemented the giant school photo with individual photos not unlike studio shots, which are offered for sale to the child's parents. This shift reflects the trend from formal to more 'personalized' family photography. The one moment in educational careers still documented in traditional ritualistic form (like weddings), is graduation from college. Millions of students continue to hire gowns for this one day; their parents can have the photo which gives proof of their achievement.

All these kinds of photos merge with family photography. The one exception is the criminal type mug-shot usually taken on entry to the institution, so that staff can identify new students. But of course they are never really just 'factual': haircut, clothes, expression, the way they write their names, all build up assumptions about students before we even meet them let alone get to know them. And the photographs required in applications, although ostensibly for identification only, are often known to affect choice of interviewees.

All the ideologies incorporated into domestic photography – democracy, choice, fun, leisure – are reproduced on a large scale in public photographs which, in modelling themselves on the family photograph's format, can more easily tap 'family values'. Any sensible politician will use a family photo rather than a mug-shot on their election hand-out. We can be relied on to sympathize with the family of the industrialist kidnapped by 'terrorists', to share the excitement of royal weddings, and interest ourselves in the children of film stars. The *forms* of 'private' photography are especially important in the public sphere to guarantee the intimacy and identification between audience and subject which a formal press-photograph could not achieve. Advertising also relies heavily on images of the family, the crucial consumers of domestic goods, although rather than following domestic photography it holds out aspirations of how families *should* look, act, and consume. These kinds of pictures make up the great bulk of advertising. But even the most unlikely campaigns will make use of the 'family album' format to familiarize their product. My favourite is the ad for an American Express card which appears to have its own family/holiday album. This advertisement seems bizarre because nothing could be further removed in ideology than the family and giant banking corporations. Yet, returning to the discussion of the State, it is precisely this separation of the family from the political and economic interests it serves that gives it such ideological value; and photography, a process developed historically alongside the modern bourgeois family, has a large place in that value. Photography offers an important, enjoyable and potentially radical access to the means of producing self-images: but as long as those images remain bound by the ideology of the family, that potential will only occasionally or accidentally be realized.

(*Ten-8*, 1984)

NOTES

1. Gramsci in the *Prison Notebooks* describes 'two major superstructural "levels": the one that can be called "civil society", that is the ensemble of organisms commonly called "private", and that of "political society" or "the State".' His distinction between the 'hegemony' exercised by the dominant group in the former sphere, and the 'direct domination' exercised by 'juridical' government in the latter, paves the way for Althusser's later differentiation between 'Ideological State Apparatuses' and 'Repressive State Apparatuses'. While the family would usually be categorized as an 'Ideological State Apparatus' in this schema, Gramsci's description of two 'levels' makes it possible to see that the family does also come under the exercise of 'juridical government': it has a foot in both levels.

2. For some good examples of this, and a more detailed discussion of the history of family photographs, see Julia Hirsch, *Family Photographs: Content, Meaning and Effect.*

3. As Walter Benjamin has pointed out ('A Short History of Photography'), the 'dignity' and 'repose' that are part of the ideological aura of early photographs derive from the length of time necessary for successsful photographic exposure. People had to stand very still as the light 'struggled painfully out of darkness' onto the plate: thus technique and ideology were as inextricably linked as they are in today's 'instant fun' Polaroid photography.

4. Walter Benjamin, *op. cit.*

HOLLYWOOD NIGHTS

Those Hollywood nights
In those Hollywood hills
She was looking so right in her diamonds and frills
Oh those big city nights in those high rolling hills
Above all the lights she had all of her skills . . .

. . . And those Hollywood nights
In those Hollywood hills
It was looking so right, it was giving him chills
In those big city nights in those high rolling hills
Above all the lights with a passion that kills

Bob Seger, from *'Hollywood Nights'*
(for The Silver Bullet Band)

TWO OR THREE THINGS WE KNOW
ABOUT OURSELVES

A Critique of *Riddles of the Sphinx* and *3 Women*

Images of women in (mainstream) films have been criticized frequently and intelligently[1], but always in relation to a *male* spectator. There is a Real, voyeuristic man, who has reactions and desires, and a Celluloid, or rather Acetate woman, who is both symbolic and an object of 'scopophilic' pleasure. Sexist images of women, sexist forms of presenting those images, are 'bad' because of their effect on *men*. Obviously I don't disagree with this. But women have to watch these same images, and *their* viewing position, or even their reactions, are rarely accounted for. The 'look' of the spectator is invariably constituted as a male look. Thus much film criticism reflects and perpetuates women's situation of having to view ourselves always through men's views of us.

My spectator is a 'she'. She is used to battling with images of motherhood, of feminine mystique, of women as jokes, of women as consumers, of inarticulate women; but it is easier to reject such images when they appear, for example, on television or in mainstream sexist cinema, than when they arise in films that claim to be different. Of the two films I am looking at, *Riddles of the Sphinx* is more obviously 'different' since it is made and distributed outside the commercial cinema, and one of its makers is a woman. However, the very title of Altman's film also makes a certain claim: at a time when the liberation of women is one of the primary issues in society, a film called *3 Women* sets itself up as belonging within that arena. In any case, a film 'about' women, rather than men, is as unusual as a film 'by' a woman. What is disturbing in both cases is the idea that this 'about' and 'by' are somehow in themselves enough, or preclude criticism. This is really a patronizing attitude, although seeming deferential: especially with *Riddles,* an element of 'being nice' is involved (a woman made it) but supporting Laura Mulvey as an independent film maker, which I do, is different from 'agreeing with' her films. And far worse, the 'compelling beauty' which one male critic finds in *3 Women* probably has to do simply with watching three attractive women. I don't want to keep lumping the two films together, because they are different in many aspects, but they are both films whose involvement with women has given them an invisible halo which only criticism from a feminist position can dispel.

Riddles of the Sphinx is the more 'serious' film, yet its very title suggests the sort of Mystery of Woman which is precisely a *male* view of women. This mysteriousness is set up in the 'stones' section with blurry shots of the Sphinx accompanied by electronic music: it almost has the aura of a Turkish Delight advertisement, 'full of Eastern Promise'. This use of the Sphinx can be seen as part of a strategy intended to evoke mystery and an image of inscrutable womanhood, as a preliminary to their 'deconstruction' with the later role of the Sphinx as a speaking subject: 'she' is given a voice. But this involves a fundamental misconception: you don't dispel a myth by trying to make it speak, or reject an image by giving it a voice with which to deny itself. The film undercuts its own strategy, by not recognizing that the power of an image of Female Mystery is so strong that it functions in the most traditional way and is *too strong to be undercut by anything later in the film* – even if this were intended. (It is in fact built on in the 'British Museum' section). Using such an image at all is to acknowledge its validity; it is already too late to deny that it 'fits'. No amount of formal strategy can undo the implicit admission of Sphinx-like mystique.

Not to realize this is to underestimate the 'autonomy' and general tenacity which is part of the nature of social symbols and which confronts the film maker trying to bend images to her own purpose. The Sphinx on the screen traverses time and space to imply that there *are* eternal qualities of women, that the questions don't change and are not determined by actual social conditions. A question is different from a riddle, anyway, since it doesn't contain its answer, while a riddle is a puzzle whose answer is found in itself and is essentially a joke. Although on the narrative level (i.e. in the Oedipus story) the Sphinx asks men questions, 'she' doesn't question men; and the connotation of the story, in which 'she' speaks, is secondary to the image in which 'she' doesn't speak but is overlaid with music. In this long showing of the Sphinx the necessity that women *ask* the questions becomes confused with the idea that women *are* the question. The Sphinx's riddle is herself. *'She'* is the eternal puzzle, unable to question actual oppression because, like real women, 'she' is not located socially but removed from history and used as a symbol, *something women have had enough of.* To assume that such a symbol 'does not have *a* meaning, but it does have meaning within the shifting contexts set up for it by the film's discourse' (to quote one review), and to see the text as only 'producing meanings' (ibid), ignores the dangers of *re*-using, *re*producing existing social meanings. Moreover the superimposition of a symbol from ancient Egyptian society onto one from our own (Greta Garbo) gives the latter an apparent inevitability. Similarly the whole Sphinx section throws a determinism over the rest of the film, mythologizing some of the real issues of the 'Louise' section.

It is in the 'Louise' section that the 'Sphinx' takes on 'a

questioning voice, a voice asking a riddle'.[2] But this inner voice, inarticulately murmuring disjointed phrases and words . . . 'Nesting . . . Acquiesced . . . Memory . . . Mystery . . .' and so on, in the 'gaps' of the written narrative, is fulfilling exactly the role expected of it by a male society with a monopoly on coherent speech. Women are left to dredge up vague impressions, to recount dreams; relegated to a kind of underworld of the unconscious. In one scene the two women sit in a womb-like room, full of red velvet curtains and rich with womanhood, surrounded by mirrors, while one of them reads out a dream neither understands. 'What does it mean? I can't understand most of it' . . . 'Pieces of thoughts I put into words. Pieces of words which seemed to mean something . . .' 'What about this? What does this mean?' . . . 'I don't know. It must be something I copied out of a book' . . . 'What does that mean, I wonder.' 'I don't know exactly. That's why I wrote it.' Women not only have a mystical, symbolic, irrational speech: it is shown as being unintelligible even to themselves. (And why is it Maxine, the black woman, who has the strange, magical dream which they cannot make sense of?) In the British Museum shots we are shown a language (Egyptian) incomprehensible not only to men but to women too. The introduction expressly describes the Sphinx as 'disordering logical categories'. All this justifies the prevailing ideological view of woman's bounteous, timeless unreason and is completely complicit with the image of women which is inscribed in male rational discourse as the representation of its opposite.

It could be argued that Laura Mulvey's speech, circumscribing the film, provides the cogency and outline for the rest of it, but this is accepting a privileged status for Laura Mulvey (whose access to a multiplicity of myths is indicated by the objects like the Greek vase, not to mention the globe, which surround her at the beginning) – and not for 'Louise', who is then 'spoken around'. Certainly Laura Mulvey's speech provides a framework for the other sections, but it is a framework which is self-negating because of what is said: most of all because of the idea that Oedipus represents the conscious, the Sphinx (Woman) the unconscious. Either this idea is not borne out by Laura Mulvey's controlling speech, or, alternatively, it makes her speech just another of these symbolic manifestations of the unconscious. It cannot work both ways: to claim the speech of unreason is to deny the speech in which you claim it. This is what terrifies me, as a woman, in the face of any such general statement about womanhood: my speech is to be invalidated in terms of rationality. It is not conscious and social but comes from murky primeval depths hardly known to myself.

The answer to this is that one rejects the very terms of patriarchal rationality. But to perpetuate even the idea of such a division as Oedipus/Male/Conscious v. Sphinx/Female/Unconscious is to be within those terms and gratefully to speak in the only 'language' they offer to women. In using this 'language' and accepting an 'inner' role women continue to be symbolic: symbolic of the otherness required by the dominant logical order. Only by rejecting this symbolic status can women regain speech. Unfortunately it becomes harder than ever to reject the role of the 'unconscious' now that the unconscious and its structures have become such a fascinating area to both men and women. Also unfortunate is the connection of the Oedipus myth with supposedly timeless unconscious structures so that motherhood and mother/child relations continue to occupy the limelight in the arena of 'womanhood'.

For here also there seems to me a mistake: the alternative to patriarchy isn't an emphasis on *motherhood*. There is a confusion between an interest *in* mothers, (for example, it is important to examine the mother-structure as well as the father-structure of patriarchy) with an interest in *being* a mother, having babies. Again, the mother-and-child image is so powerful that no amount of family-breakdown-campaigning-for-nursery-schools narrative in the rest of the film is going to undermine it : all the classic connotations right down to Madonna-images are inevitably evoked. Laura Mulvey says that in our society 'the place of the mother is suppressed', but this is just not true, it is exalted into the *only* possible place for women. In *Riddles* motherhood seems a mysterious and fulfilling experience (despite the horror of having to part with baby when he/she goes to nursery) which excludes not only men but women who are not mothers. It is interesting that at the point of actual campaigning for day-care nurseries the narrative fizzles out into a brief dialogue concerning problems in the unions: we are not *shown* this struggle but we *are* shown mother-and-child images, over and over.

This is particularly claustrophobic because the title and framework of the film give an implied universality to everything in it: it clearly sets out to be about womanhood in general, yet most of its images are those that women have been fighting for years, and its ground is marked out within the most traditional 'women's' areas – babies, bodies, feelings, vague memories, dreams, mystery – but now part of some sort of Lacanian theory. Women are never shown actually *producing* anything except babies; and there is a potential voyeurism in the 'jugglers' acrobatic sequence, which is so visually attractive. I felt oppressed by my own implied inclusion in all this: it did not seem to be a film *for* women, for we don't need to be told what areas we represent ('the unconscious'). So it seemed, rather, addressed to men: why represent traditional womanhood to women? We are struggling *not* to recognize ourselves in such images.

The 'women's areas' which, it could be argued, *Riddles of the Sphinx* at least attempts to investigate, are all brought into play far more crudely in *3 Women*, where the *pregnant* woman with long dark hair (Janice Rule) is a distillation of all the qualities discussed above: she is almost completely silent all through the film, wild and witch-like, so full of creativity with her 'primitive' paintings and earth-motherhood. She is a mute, all-pervasive presence, only able to communicate through her art. Despite her having less screen-time and dialogue than the others, the image of this woman is central to the film and is set against the blustering 'male chauvinist pig' pseudo-cowboy, who is so caricatured as to subtly deny real manifestations of sexism.

The other two women are also almost caricatures. A great deal of the humour surrounding the Shelley Duval figure is at her own expense, particularly directed at her consumer-ism. Examined closely these are really snide little jokes about 'taste' and people who eat canned food and buy frilly furnishings. No attempt is made to suggest why this woman should feel the need for such stereotyped consumption. The other main 'joke' is the pathetic lies she tells about her social and sexual life. Her rejection by men is somehow made into a failing of *hers*. To make fun of such symptoms of oppression is appalling.

Having represented mystic artistic pregnant womanhood, and 'silly' instant-food buying magazine-reading woman-hood, all that is left to represent is naive girlishness: the Sissy Spacek figure, Pinkie. That these are the only options for women is indicated by the role *reversal* that takes place after Pinkie's suicide attempt. The underwater paintings which hover through the film and the apparently meaning-less 'dream' sequence, which is simply a mish-mash of previous shots and images, seem to relegate the whole drama to the 'unconscious' level and the narrative events themselves are, as 'story', so improbable a heaping up of loaded meanings (adultery, suicide, childbirth, shooting etc) that one has to fall back on the idea of a 'psychological drama' in an attempt to make any sense of it. Yet on this level what is most strongly suggested is that women are crazy – all they can apparently do is choose different ways to be crazy. Miss Naiveté becomes the Hard Woman, while Miss

Commercial becomes Mrs. Motherly, but this role swapping makes no attempt to locate the social origin and function of the roles. We are shown apparently unstable, neurotic women but no causes for their behaviour, and often, indeed, with the suggestion that it is all very endearing, as when Shelley Duval keeps shutting her skirt in the car door or Pinkie washes her underwear and we snigger our way into women's privacy.

Not so endearing are the women who are made to stand for the oppression which is actually practised by *men, against* women: the nasty, bossy nurse at the hospital and the terrifying woman who supervises work at the geriatric baths. This film shows an interest in institutions characteristic of much American cinema, and characteristically defined without reference to class. What happens in this case is that any manifestation of a dominant class is replaced by women. This shows classic male paranoia of the kind embodied in the 'Nurse Ratchett' figure in *One Flew Over the Cuckoo's Nest*; a typical example of a large repressive institution represented through one dominating woman. This is always very sexist, but to have bossy women oppressing the 'heroines' in *3 Women* locates both the feminist *and* the class struggle as being between *women*: they are just *nasty* to one another. There is no real engagement with men except the symbolic Cowboy; and it seems to be Shelley Duval's fault that Pinkie jumps suicidally into the pool. It is a dangerous internalization of real struggle, making it internal *among* women – quite as dangerous as the more obvious internalization resulting from its location in the female unconscious, as in *Riddles of the Sphinx*.

The most disturbing case of women 'filling' existing oppressive institutions is the reversion to a 'family' structure at the end, where the three women have settled down into classic family roles after excluding men from their lives. Since this is hardly an attempt at 'realism' (after all, women *are* nurses, but they are never *fathers*) it appears to be making some symbolic point, but what point? What is being said about the family and about women? This is not a film about the family as such; the only 'real' family is Pinkie's parents who are again caricatured. Rather it is a 'Family Romance'[3]: the components of the cast are rearranged to form a new family structure, Pinkie having denied that her parents are related to her and found a surrogate in Shelley Duval. This ending would seem to imply that the family structure is irreplaceable. Otherwise why could not the three women just live together like adults? The ending seems significant but is simply irresponsible, like a punch-line that cannot be understood. Altman has a peculiar penchant for picking areas that are fashionably political (cf *M.A.S.H.*) and then merely playing around in them. That a film about women can be seen as commercially viable at all in the US is a tribute to the growth and strength of the women's movement there: *3 Women* can only be seen like this, as a symptom, not as a valid investigation of any kind. As usual, little has been said of its relation to the woman viewer, but how can a woman read this film? If she sees something of herself in the women depicted, she seems to accept the determinism of the roles involved, and alternatively if she joins in the jokes about convenience-foods and lonely single women she is having a superior laugh about other women. This is another film which by being 'about' women excludes real women: the choice between identification and detachment is a false one since both equally involve a positioning, the latter being the more dangerous because it invites us to 'see through' the characters *as though they were real* (like noticing the skirt shut in the car door). Altman offers the woman viewer a male position of amused, sympathetic criticism and *superior knowledge* to the 'women' in the film, and this position must be fought because the very images of women offered in the film are false.

If there is one thing women don't need, it is images of Woman. We don't need the eternal myth-status which both

LES SECRETS

The night holds a secret every woman can share.

Night is the time to take special care of your complexion, a time to discover the secret of younger looking skin.

While you sleep, Night of Ulay Enriched Beauty Cream will ease away dryness, and replace the moisture so vital to your skin's health and beauty.

A unique blend of oils and emollients, it is quickly and completely absorbed, leaving your skin smoother, softer.

Light and non-greasy, yet rich and nourishing, Night of Ulay will help keep your skin young looking.

The secret of younger looking skin.

'explains' and is a reparation for our exclusion from the affairs of particular, historical societies, a status held out by the Sphinx and by the silent artist in *3 Women*. We don't need the traditional images of motherhood abounding in both films. But it is easy to see why there has been such a surge of interest in the *psychology* of womanhood rather than in day-to-day oppression and the social status of women. For hundreds of years there has been what Michèle Le Doeuff describes as an 'imaginary portrait of "woman", a power of disorder nocturnal, a dark beauty, a black continent, sphinx of dissolution, the depths of the unintelligible, mouthpiece of the underworld gods, an internal enemy who corrupts and perverts without any sign of combat, a place where all forms fade away.'[4] What has changed in recent years is *not the identification of 'woman' with all these things but the value placed on them by male discourse.* With the so-called discovery of a language of the unconscious, women have, sadly, seized on something they may call their own, and taking this as 'their' area, have espoused a potential determinism with all the ardour of a proud housewife who assumes total command of the only area allowed her. At last, it seems, women have something going for them – unreason has ceased to be 'bad', and psychoanalytic theories are in fashion. But while challenging patriarchal structures of thought and society it is crucial not to do so from the position already embedded in those structures, and we want absolutely nothing to do with the sort of underworld femininity they offer us. As Le Doeuff goes on to say, 'women, real women, have no need to be concerned by that femininity; we are continuously compared with that image but we do not have to recognize ourselves in it . . . As soon as one considers this femininity as an illusory reject from conflicts within the field of reason assimilated to masculinity, it is out of the question to try to let it express itself. We will not talk pidgin to please the colonialists.'

Yet that is what I believe *Riddles* does, and more dangerously than *3 Women* in that at least the Altman can make no claim to be women's speech. His film offers a 'colonial' view of the 'natives', tempered with a certain sympathetic interest which is the direct result of a concrete social battle for recognition. But the implication of *Riddles* is the equivalent of looking for the roots of colonial oppression in 'native' consciousness, locating both the struggle and its solution in the inner lives of the oppressed. 'To the patriarchy, the Sphinx as woman is a riddle': but women do not need to see themselves through the eyes of the patriarchy and be a riddle to themselves. We need to claim consciousness, not unconsciousness. In patriarchy women may be 'the equivalent of a sign which is being communicated'[5], but we have no time to waste decoding that sign as though it were capable of revealing us to ourselves.

(1977)

NOTES

1. Laura Mulvey's own article 'Visual Pleasure and Narrative Cinema' is one of the most lucid and important on this topic.

2. This and all the following quotations from the film are taken from the script of *Riddles of the Sphinx* by Peter Wollen and Laura Mulvey, published in *Screen*.

3. Family Romance: 'phantasies by means of which the subject invents a new family for himself, and in doing so works out a sort of romance.' Laplanche & Pontalis, *The Language of Psychoanalysis* p.160.

4. This quotation and the following are taken from an excellent article on 'Women and Philosophy', in *Radical Philosophy* no.17.

5. Juliet Mitchell, *Psychoanalysis and Feminism* p.371.

NICE GIRLS DO

Why does Doris Day 'deserve' a major season at the National Film Theatre? Why is she the subject of an 80-page dossier from the British Film Institute? Why is an actress with a 'virgin-next-door' image being 'reclaimed' by feminists? Why does she warrant a two-page magazine feature?

Each time I have had to answer these questions it has become more apparent that Doris Day is remembered in a certain way: as the boring 'Good' girl, who hung on to her virginity through thick and thin; as the wholesome, All-American heroine of the '50s who embodies everything the 'liberated' '60s generation set itself against; and by film-buffs, as the dated star of some hammy musical comedies – 'women's films', but not good cinema.

The determination to see Day as the 'clean, unsexy' stereotype with little serious significance, is a fascinating phenomenon: because few of these presumptions are borne out by the films themselves. In a 20-year career Day made 39 films, including thrillers, melodramas, and sophisticated sex comedies, in which she plays roles as diverse as a lobster farmer and a night-club singer. Her more conventional social roles, where she's 'just' a wife, are in the thrillers; where in each case she is subjected to violence from men – in three cases, from her husband. In the lighter films, she almost invariably plays an independent working woman (teacher, shop steward in a pyjama factory, lumber-yard owner), whose involvement in her work, and independence of thought, are presented in direct contradiction with the ideas of the men who want her, and expect her to fall mindlessly into their arms. She resists not sex, but submission: 'Just because I kissed you, does that make me your girl?' (*Pajama Game*, 1957). And where she does figure as a girl-next-door in suburbia (e.g. *Young at Heart*, 1955) she fails to fulfil expectations and on the day of her wedding to the 'boy-next-door' figure, elopes with the cynical, suicidal Frank Sinatra.

The discrepancy between the *image* of Day and her actual films raises much more interesting questions than those about Day 'herself'. How is the star's image 'fixed' in a way that can exclude many of her film roles? Why is the kind of woman Day plays so often (funny, independent, bright) seen as not sexy (whereas Marilyn Monroe, from the same era and with no greater acting ability, now has a great following)? Why are these kinds of films so scornfully regarded as 'dated'? Is there a vested interest in 'forgetting' the many problems and conflicts raised in them?

All stars and public figures have images which are lop-sided and partial, but women, whether stars or not, are subject to sets of images which are mutually exclusive: the clever, 'unfeminine' girl/the dumb blonde; the good wife and mother/the nymphet, etc. In another '50s film, *The Girl Can't Help It* (1956) the punchline is that sex-bomb Jayne Mansfield actually *loves* fixing turkey dinners and keeping house: the fact that it's meant to be amazing shows how these qualities are seen as opposites. And what oppositions of this sort have in common is the separation of sexuality from other qualities. Since when were 'nice' men not sexy? Or sexy men 'dumb'?

Taken together, the images of Doris Day and Marilyn

Monroe (who were equally successful) can be seen as a manifestation of precisely this split: Monroe is 'dumb, innocent, sexy' while Day is 'freckled, pert, wholesome'. On the literal level, it was the publicity machine at Warner Brothers which 'created' her clean, sunshiney image: stills always show her smiling (smiling isn't sexy – look at the pouting models in any magazine) and decently dressed – but it was her role as a *mother* which endowed her with virtue and cleanliness (though clearly not virginity!). A typical publicity still shows her scrubbing behind her small son's ears: 'Between her Warner Bros screen career, co-starring on the weekly Bob Hope radio broadcast, and satisfying the demands of fans the world over, blonde singing star Doris Day is a pretty busy young lady – but never too busy to neglect her duties and pleasures as mother to 7-year-old Terry.' Warners may have plugged this image, but the attitudes already existed which ensured it popular currency. (This was the era of Bowlby's influential theories on the necessity of *mothering*, etc). Audiences adored the 'girl-next-door' figure and were disturbed by anything out of 'character' – as when Day received thousands of letters from fans distressed by her role as Ruth Etting, the night-club singer raped by her lover (James Cagney) in *Love Me Or Leave Me* (1955). Most of the rape scene was cut, which Day herself regarded as 'chickening out'.

This was by no means the only 'dark' film of Day's. How about *Storm Warning* (1951) in which Day is married to a Klu Klux Klan member who shoots her and tries to rape her sister? Or *Midnight Lace* (1960) where Day plays a wife persecuted by threatening phone calls, which turn out to be from her husband, trying to drive her to suicide? When this film ran on TV recently, it was announced as 'a tense, psychological thriller set in London during the famous fogs of the 50s, starring Rex Harrison, and, *in an untypical dramatic role, Doris Day.*' The final image of the film, Day walking towards camera with tears on her face, was

Above: Monroe, The Seven Year Itch
Right: Day, The Pajama Game

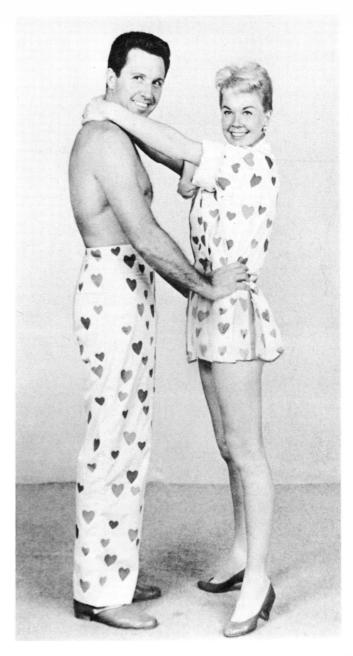

hurriedly replaced with a still of the 'famous grin' and the assurance that 'Doris Day can be seen *in a more familiar role* later this season when the BBC will be showing a season of Doris Day musicals.'

This perpetual attempt to pin down the image of Day as sunny and straightforward shows that something must be at stake: the public image could not be contradictory. With Day's own life, her motherhood was stressed, but her two earlier, unhappy marriages were concealed – just as recent news has shown that a TV personality and Mayor's wife cannot be an insecure woman who shoplifts. The possibility of contradictions within public figures threatens the status quo, because if people are capable of inconsistency and change, so is the whole of society.

Change, and the remoulding of sexual roles, are at the centre of most of Day's films. In the sex comedies the plot always involves change on both sides, but for Day, this is usually an increasing sexual attraction for the man, while *he* is forced to modify his world view in accordance with her social outlook. In *The Pajama Game* Day plays a shop steward involved in a battle for a 7½ cent per hour rise. The new, young factory supervisor falls for her: 'If we love each other, nothing can come between us'. But she, *although equally 'in love'*, warns him: '7½ cents is going to come between us. The contract is important to me . . . no matter what's with us, I'm going to be fighting for my side and fighting hard.' There is no happy ending for the love story until he has come round to backing the workers' claim. In *Teacher's Pet* (1958) Clark Gable is made to rethink his cynical ideas about the role of education – and about sexual stereotypes, as he assumes the 'least attractive' woman in the classroom to be the teacher – and is stunned to find that it's blonde, high-heeled Doris Day who is 'Professor Stone'.

The questioning of sexual roles *during* these films is partially undercut by the endings, where invariably the antagonists pair off, and the Day figure loses her (material) independence. We are given no reason to assume she ⟍ lose her independence of mind: still, the fact that she is 'brought round' at all can be seen as reassurance to the male ego. But it is a peculiar feature of films that often the image you are left with is not the *final* one. *Calamity Jane* (1953) may be frilled up and married off after 101 minutes, but she can equally be remembered as the buckskin-clad stagecoach guard of the first hour and a half.

Which image is 'remembered' depends on what's in it for you, and what the current set of ideas about women happens to be. The 1950s emphasis on Day's healthy young mother image was bound up with the renewed stress on family life after the social upheaval of the Second World War. The desire for a reassuring picture of the 'girl-next-door', with an unthreatening sexuality, was clearly strong enough at this time to produce a particular, selective viewing of Day's films. The notions of balance between the male and female protagonists in the comedies, and the 'civilizing' effect of the female's ideas on the man, demonstrate another aspect of '50s thought: that men and women were 'Equal but Different' in their domestic and social roles.

If '50s ideas about femininity produced the first 'repression' of issues raised in Day films, the '60s era of 'liberation' put the lid on them completely. The fact that most of the Day characters battle for their own views to be accepted before 'giving' themselves sexually was forgotten as the advent of the Pill made *any* reason for saying 'No' seem out of date; and another partial view of Day, the 'Constant Virgin', developed. It is interesting that in 1967 Day turned down the part of Mrs Robinson in *The Graduate* not because it was a sexual role but because the way it depicted sexual relations was exploitative – an evaluation many feminists would now agree with. But by the late '60s the Day image was on its way out, no longer corresponding to a popular mythology of women. And the demise of the Hollywood studio system at around the same time meant that the kind of stars who had held such sway as public idols for over four decades were on the way out for good.

So why are women, particularly, becoming interested in Doris Day films again? Perhaps the decade of films that followed the end of her career has something to do with it. The post-'68 years provided us with films like *Midnight Cowboy, Easy Rider, A Clockwork Orange, Straw Dogs, Dirty Harry, The Collector, Five Easy Pieces, The Sting, Butch Cassidy* – not a period noted for its variety and scope in female characters. And there is no equivalent of the Day figure even in contemporary 'women's' films (*An Unmarried Woman, The Turning Point, Girlfriends,* etc) which lack the humour and vitality of the successful 'genre' films (musicals, sex comedies etc) of the '50s. The ground of earlier 'women's films', domestic comedy and 'weepies', has now moved into TV: it's no coincidence that the BBC is running their current Day season in a 6.30 weekday slot – competing with the daily soap opera *Crossroads*.

Reclaiming Day's films in no way means disowning this connection – or this audience. It means claiming the *validity* of the apparently trivial struggles at work and in personal relationships, which are still regarded as 'women's areas' (as opposed to the dramatically macho terrain of most popular cinema). Most of all it means welcoming any image, for they are scarce enough, of a woman who steers her way through these struggles with generosity, humour and self-respect. Day never played the part of a character who knowingly betrayed her own principles. This may sound old-fashioned, but at a time when so many movies, not to mention the ruling political climate, are more brutal than ever, it is a policy and a group of films not to be sneered at.

(First published as 'Reclaim the Day', *Time Out*, 1980)

PRISONER OF LOVE

Beautifully shot, breathtakingly accurate, Raging Bull *goes still further into the territory Scorsese has mapped in all his films – men and male values; in this case through the story of 1949 middleweight champion Jake LaMotta. De Niro's performance as the cocky young boxer who gradually declines into a pathetic fat slob forces you to question the rigid and sentimental codes of masculinity which he clings to even as they destroy him, like a drowning man clutching a lead weight. His blind jealousy of his wife, the pride and inability to communicate which keep him locked in a feud with his brother, are made literally unattractive as Jake himself becomes physically, as well as emotionally gross. Certain gestures are unforgettable: Jake fiddling in frustration with a TV set, the swagger round the ring after beating an opponent to pulp. The anti-realism of the fights – brilliantly shot and cut – prevents them sinking back into the narrative and instead creates a set of images which resound through Jake's personal confrontations: their smashing, story-less violence is relentlessly cut with domestic scenes until you learn to flinch in anticipation. This film does more than just make you think about how men act – it makes you* see *it. (JW)* – Review, Time Out

Raging Bull is hardly likely to win Martin Scorsese the Sensitive Male Film-Maker of the Year award. It has already aroused much hostility. A picture about a strutting, obsessive boxing champion whose every gesture seems to embody all that the modern liberation-seeker casts out in disgust, a picture with repeated scenes of almost unbearable violence, appears to offer little to the Caring Person, the Concerned About Relationships, those striving to avoid the nastier aspects of masculinity in themselves or others. For here they are, flung at your face, those unfashionable qualities like rage, jealousy, paranoia, and also blind desire. But do liberating films have to show liberated people?

Talking of liberated men, Jake La Motta (Robert de Niro), the boxing hero of *Raging Bull,* certainly *isn't.* La Motta was 'The Bronx Bull', the 1949 middleweight champion who later fell from grace: a nightclub owner in Miami, he was sent to jail for allowing juvenile prostitutes on the premises, and wound up in the Bronx as a strip-club comic, where he recited speeches from Shakespeare to Tennessee Williams. (One of his favourites was Marlon Brando's famous confession from *On The Waterfront:* 'I coulda been a contender, Charlie . . .'). As a fighter he was famed for having an unusually thick skull.

In a central scene from the film, Jake is in his living room with his brother, trying to get a picture on the TV. His wife Vikki is upstairs. As he messes with the faulty set, Jake's huge, powerful body is useless, and his pent-up frustration builds at this thing he can't make work by hitting – like his home life.

Confronted with something too complex to be bent to his will in the only way he knows, Jake goes berserk on a quite different tack. His suspicions rise to an accusation of his brother: 'You fucked my wife? You fucked my wife?' 'You ask me that, your own brother? You expect me to answer that?' Both are outraged with a sentimental concern for their own pride that's peculiarly masculine. Jake goes upstairs to his wife. His insane jealousy takes the form of both physical obsession with what he imagines to have happened – 'You sucked his cock?' – and physical revenge. In the culmination of the episode he beats up both his wife and his brother.

The success of *Raging Bull* in *not* just showing more male violence lies in the fact that the TV-set build-up is inseparable from the whole sequence, and creates, not the sense of Jake's strength, but of his impotence.

When, in another scene, Vikki observes idly that a young contender has a pretty face, Jake can't rest until he's knocked the boy's nose half way to his ear, in one of the film's most brutal boxing scenes: 'He ain't pretty no more.' But again, instead of power we feel the inadequacy of using the ring to work out a paranoid personal obsession.

These connections and comparisons between feelings and images are aided by the black-and-white photography, the slow motion, and the *lack* of realism (contrary to the publicity) in the fights: a film in the more familiar colour, told like a realistic story, might perhaps glorify what the more formalistic *Raging Bull* presents as contradictory.

For, although Jake sounds like one big shit so far, what should we make of the film's very tender love scenes? After Jake has beaten up Vikki and his brother in the scene described above, he enters the bedroom to apologize as she's packing to leave. When he finally stops saying sorry and touches her, she lets the pile of clothes drop from her arm and turns to him . . . This sensual scene of *mutual* physical passion prevents their relationship being reduced to one of simple oppression.

Jake himself cannot be reduced either, simply to an example of how not to be. Like so many of Scorsese's heroes, his masculinity is in crisis, riven by explosive passions and impossible desires. Jake La Motta is literally a tragic figure; for the same thing which makes him great – his body – can destroy him.

The crucial role played by his body in the meaning of

Raging Bull is shown by the fact that de Niro put on 60 pounds for the film's latter sequences, ruining his own physique in the process. With its central character fundamentally inarticulate, the film, like La Motta, has to find physical forms of expression. Jake's painful destruction through his own frustrated energies is *felt* as he hurls himself against the walls of his prison cell; the poignancy of his clumsy passion for his wife is *visible* in the love scene where his bloated, lumbering body is a parody of its former beauty (seen in slow motion in his leopard-skin dressing-gown) or its hideous destructiveness (pummelling an opponent's face to pulp).

Scorsese himself is no tough guy ('I don't punch people in the face. I'm too short, and I can't run – I've got asthma. So I talk my way out of things, I guess.') Asked about the presentation of masculinity in the film, he said, 'The film's the complete opposite of macho. The essence of it is that we *are* macho . . . but it's a matter of turning it inside out. Bobby and I never really intended to do that kind of thing, but we did it by doing this inside thing that we know. We did it as honestly as we know how. There's no point in doing anything else.

'At a certain point in your life you realize something's there that's part of your background, part of your make-up. That you *can't deny*. You have to be honest with that. You have to deal with what are called the "negative" aspects. You have to claw your way through them. Maybe, if there is a criticism to be made, it's too negative. People are always saying I'm too hard on myself. Maybe so. I feel something from making this picture that closes off a whole area, and that's that . . .

'Emotionally it's very difficult for me to go on doing things like *Raging Bull*. People say, "It's only a movie". But it's not that. It happens to be a movie, because that's the way you're expressing it. It could be a painting or the way you make a sandwich. So I'm not asking anyone to go and sit through my primal situation. That's what it's about. They should know that's what they're gonna be in for.'

This may be what they're in for, but it's all too comfortable to dismiss a film like *Raging Bull,* or perhaps especially the films like *Mean Streets* and *Taxi Driver,* by seeing their disturbing qualities as the film-maker's hangups. Much has been written about Scorsese's background (raised in New York's Little Italy, could have been a gangster but wanted to be a priest), but the feelings and conflicts he shows in his films aren't confined to him, and must touch a raw nerve in most audiences. There has been little serious criticism of his work which confronts *what* he is dealing with – perhaps because it is something too close to home. Why has *Raging Bull* aroused such indignant moral criticism? Why was *New York, New York* a box-office flop?

Unlike *Raging Bull, New York, New York* focuses not on one man, but on the relationship between a man and a woman (de Niro and Liza Minnelli) in a way that is strikingly honest. The gradual transition from de Niro's insistent demand for the woman he wants, to his desire to escape from a relationship which he finds restrictive, his babyish attitudes, his inability to *understand* what he feels – all these are shown in relation to another person: the woman who at first resists him but becomes increasingly unhappy and dependent as he withdraws, finally regaining her own energy and ambition as their relationship collapses. It's a depressing picture, but a familiar one. And it's the accuracy of so many gestures, conflicts, phrases, that strikes below the belt. As Minnelli lies in hospital after having the baby he doesn't want, de Niro comes in, fucked up, lost (how about her?) and cries on her lap – demanding, even at this stage when he's drawing away from her, that he be the only baby, filling the centre stage.

So why are these films often criticized not as 'films' – since they're brilliantly made – but on the 'moral' grounds that Scorsese has a yen for Macho, that in nakedly showing certain attitudes he is somehow advocating them? The only film where this point may be valid is *Taxi Driver,* where the murkier side of masculinity gets way out of control. The most violent image in it is not cinematic, but verbal, and is spoken by Scorsese himself, playing the cameo role of a jealous husband in the back of a cab threatening vengeance on his unfaithful wife: 'Did you ever see what a .44 can do to a woman's pussy, cabbie? I'm going to put it right up to her, cabbie. Right in her, cabbie . . .' Reactions to the horror of that scene are so ambivalent that even years later Scorsese is still surprised: 'A lot of famous guys come over to me and say "I love it when you say that line" . . . It's amazing. I'm embarrassed, because it slipped out by accident.'

It hardly needs to be said that this is horrible and deeply shocking. *Raging Bull* also is packed with possessive, violent and belittling attitudes towards women. But the film makes you *see* these, and gives an insight into the central male character that could never be produced if such things were suppressed. Should films show the world as it ought to be or as it is? For what seems to be demanded more nowadays by those with ideals of liberation is a cinema of the superego: as if to make a 'sensitive' or 'progressive' film now, you have to show people *being* sensitive and progressive. There is a scene in Alain Tanner's *Jonah: Who Will Be 25 In The Year 2000* (a film packed with sensitive post-marxist men and terribly pretty women) in which two men have a conversation as they peel potatoes in a kitchen. An invisible arrow points from the corner of the frame: 'This is how you should be . . . this film is not chauvinist and oppressive because we show the men peeling the potatoes . . .' It's presented so smugly, so righteously, that in watching the film some of its ideological soundness actually seems to rub off on its viewers. You *feel* progressive.

But it is also *repressive,* this desire for cleaned-up images of oneself and the world. Change certainly doesn't come through denial, even though it feels comfortably non-sexist to watch two women hitch-hike round Switzerland doing nothing, or a left-handed one sitting round the house looking elegiacally serene for no apparent reason. Cleaning up the screen doesn't necessarily help anyone clean up their act: it's precisely repression, a refusal to face things, that produces violence – as in *Raging Bull*. It's no wonder that so many movies now seem to offer one of two choices: either exploiting mindless male aggression for easy shock value, or subduing it, neutering it, pretending it just doesn't exist. Those things which 'slip out' in Scorsese's films may not be fashioned by him into a deliberately moral shape, but they do force you to confront unpleasant and awkward realities in yourself.

Pauline Kael has said that Scorsese confuses cinema with church. But despite his Calvinist script-writer (Paul Schrader), Scorsese's religious mode isn't the puritan ideal, it's the confessional: dig deep for it, churn it out, tell it in sinful and erotic detail. Instead of judging what comes out, his films focus on the energy itself; and, moving out of the realm of right and wrong, they show how that energy can either celebrate or destroy.

'That repressed energy eventually has to come out. It may go the wrong way (Scorsese bursts into laughter) . . . but it's not a good way to be to yourself. Bresson in *Diary of a Country Priest* says God is our torturer, but wants us to be merciful with ourselves. He's right. But I wish I could live that way.'

Instead of drawing spiritual conclusions though, Scorsese invests spirit into everyday events, sometimes through sex, but always through music. Every film he's made has had the quality of a musical; not with the trappings of chorus lines and song-and-dance routines, but in its essence: charging the most mundane events of a hateful daily life with motion, energy and passion. Walking down the street, catching the subway, hanging out in a bar, take on the electric intensity of desire. Even moments like getting up or going to sleep – in

Mean Streets, a man moves his head off the pillow and you hear the crashing opening drum-beats of the Ronettes' 'Be My Baby'. 'They just say "watch out" . . . musical, mad, mad opera, crazy . . . but that's the way it is . . .'. We're a long way from the bland withdrawal from daily rhythms in, say, a Wim Wenders movie – which isn't so much a musical as a vacuum pack.

Maybe it's coincidence, but Travis the psycho in *Taxi Driver* just doesn't listen to music. 'The sense of the first shots of *Taxi Driver* (yellow cab moving through New York streets at night) came out of listening to 'T.B. Sheets' by Van Morrison. We wanted it fading in and out of the whole picture with lines like . . . "foreign bodies" . . . "steppin' out" . . . "turn up the radio, turn up the radio" . . . "Gotta go" . . . just slipping in and out like a dream. That's how I got the first image. Then I realized I couldn't do it, because Travis wouldn't listen to music.'

So what's at stake in all this? Just nostalgia for adolescent frenzy? A possibility Scorsese admits when he says 'Oh God, it seems as if I'm stuck in a period of around 1961 to 1964'. Maybe *Mean Streets* really is just a punk's *American Graffiti,* anguish and despair set in motion to those oldies but goodies, the Marvelettes, the Shirelles, the Miracles, the Chantells. But apart from wondering why Scorsese just gets music that's so much *better* into his movies, it boils down to this: his people cling on to music and dreams – anything which will save them from the imminent prospect of drowning. They move through these things, sharing a common language of emotions and problems, but it doesn't help solve them. Cut off from that dream they lose the craziness and longing that make life liveable; but with it, their every action is a mystery to them, illogical and inexplicable. As in La Motta's favourite song 'Prisoner of Love', they're trapped by the very thing that inspires them. And without figuring why they just go round in circles.

Scorsese: 'What's interesting is that a very, very famous

American rock musician . . . poet, turned to Robbie Robertson when he said I was going to record *The Last Waltz* on film, and said "What's Scoresese doing it for? All he does is make pictures about how women fuck over men." I mean the guy who said this is extremely . . . he's one of the greats (reverential stare and tone of awe of the unnamable – it could only be Dylan he had in mind). But the point is I don't do that.'

Us: 'And there we were thinking how they were about how men fuck over women.'

Scorsese: 'Yeah. I mean it's much more complicated than that.'

(*Raging Bull* provoked such controversy when previewed that Rank, the distributor, refused to open it. This article, written in collaboration with Don Macpherson on the basis of our interview with Scorsese, was first published as 'A Sense of Outrage', *Time Out*, 1981)

CITY OF WOMEN

Fellini's *City of Women* is a fantastic voyage through a man's unconscious, a string of symbolic encounters and elaborate images held together with the logic of a dream. Marcello Mastroianni is perfect as Snaporaz, the superficially mild, typical well-dressed middle-aged man whose bizarre adventures/fantasies (which are the film) are triggered off by his desire for a woman in his railway carriage. He pursues her to a feminist convention, which he at first explores – through antiphallic workshops with women earnestly shouting 'we must defeat fellatio' to a large meeting with genuinely moving speeches made by older women who cast off the stigma of 'ageing' – and then tries to escape, himself pursued by a boiler-woman who tries to rape him, and by hordes of teenage girls. This leads him to the retreat of Zubercock, the last bastion of old-fashioned masculinity (for women rule the world outside), a decadent womanizer whose phallic castle boasts a gallery of talking pin-ups. Here at a party Snaporaz meets his wife, who criticizes his role in their marriage . . . and then in bed he takes off down the rollercoaster of memory, past sexual images from childhood – and cinema.

The events go rambling on, but are much less chaotic in their meaning than it appears: Fellini's circus style, a

164

succession of extravagant acts, is exactly suited to the dream-like function of turning thoughts into visual forms. As in a dream, the events speak not of themselves but of the dreamer. Real people, real places appear; but it is an internal landscape which is being projected. And just as it is always a wish which shapes the particular forms of a dream, so the emotional qualities of a film are not inherent in the filmed objects themselves, nor even in their fictional attributes, but are those of the drive which underlies it. Snaporaz's movement through the film is fuelled by desire, and fear; gradually it becomes clear that the women are externalizations of his own emotions, as with the extremely sexy but violently intimidating woman on the train, who is in fact a stranger. She is *so* sexy, and *so* stern, that it is impossible not to see these aspects of 'her' as aspects of *him,* turned inside out.

So it would be a mistake to criticize Fellini for portraying women as sex-objects, or feminists as aggressive: he is doing deliberately what other directors often do less clearly: show women through the threatened eyes of Post-Feminist Male Consciousness. This post-feminist consciousness is also the theme of, for example, Godard's *Slow Motion (Sauve Qui Peut – La Vie);* his mysteriously sexy and independent women are no less male inventions than Fellini's grosser visions – they simply appear as more realistic characters, the products of observation, rather than fantasy. Most narrative films within both mainstream and 'Art' cinema give the illusion that their characters are relatively autonomous. But while Godard's control of the strings is more concealed, Fellini really goes to town on visual means for revealing the flimsy construction of female figures in film. Towards the end of *City of Women* Snaporaz is chasing the image of the Ideal Woman: she turns out to be a larger-than-life inflated dummy, and as he floats off into the sky clinging to this giant balloon, her 'real' counterpart on the ground below fires a shot which crumples his dream and brings our hero down to earth.

Ultimately *City of Women* is about cinema, the way it *is* a dream, and very much a sexual one. Recent feminist film theory centres on the idea of male desire: Fellini concretizes this in one image – a huge bed which is the cinema, full of boys sharing the wet-dream of a woman on the screen. Images like this must surely have a powerful meaning for feminists, as well as Fellini fans.

(Spare Rib, 1981)

SUBVERSIVE SITUATIONS

There is a limit to the time you can spend wondering whose body is in a swimming pool, and when we reached that limit early last summer my friends and I turned our Saturday night attention to *Flamingo Road*. This much-maligned programme rapidly became an even more crucial date than *Dallas* had been. You can tell that it's become very popular because the BBC change its time every week and sometimes skip it altogether; treatment the TV stations keep especially for one's favourites.

Programmed in *Dallas'* old slot, *Flamingo Road* was clearly intended to satisfy the same appetite for serialized melodrama that *Dallas* had fed. This TV genre could be described as 'sit-drama' – the 'sit' in question being patriarchy. Both *Dallas* and *Flamingo Road* are centred on corrupt, powerful patriarchs who dominate business and personal relations. JR is of course famous, and has even spawned commercial by-products, like JR after-shave and 'I hate JR' beakers. His counterpart in *Flamingo Road* is Sheriff Titus Semple, always just called Titus, who looks exactly like Colonel Sanders of Kentucky Fried Chicken – even to the ridiculous necktie. Both programmes are *about* power, and are fuelled by the almost voyeuristic, post-Watergate American delight in watching, having laid bare, the mechanisms of corruption. Voyeuristic because, while one disapproves, one still delights in looking. But this exposure of patriarchal power can also be radical.

I would argue that it is slightly *less* so in *Dallas*, although the programme's construction is *more* radical in that you don't identify with anyone in it. The characters are all obnoxious in their own ways: you just watch their re-arrangements and wheelings and dealing. It *shows* patriarchal power in personal relationships, but never poses an alternative to the stereotypes it deals in: the only women who ever threatened JR were Kirsten, the most objectionable little creep in the world, and Leslie, the woman with dazzling white hair who, Thatcher-like, matched his business cunning with her own.

Flamingo Road showed a different style, even from the theme music: *Dallas'* announces itself brashly, almost like a military bugle; *Flamingo Road's,* with its trailing lead-in phrase, is like the anecdotal start of a first-person novel. And the first person to prove a real novelty in this new series was its heroine, Lane Ballou. Leaving a shadier life in a travelling fair, Lane Ballou hit Truro (small-town Florida) as both a sexual and political threat to the status quo. She and Titus' deputy fell for each other: unfortunately the deputy, Field, was engaged to marry the daughter of a wealthy industrialist, so Lane's sexual role involved, from the start, a disruption of the business order and allegiances of Truro. Titus got her out of the way – in prison on a trumped-up charge, Field thought she'd left him and married the awful Constance: thereby setting up the scenario of a loveless marriage, and the tensions – will Lane and Field get back together?

But Lane's threat involved far more than being – potentially – the Other Woman to Field's marriage. She was in a way the Other Woman to the whole pattern of womanhood in Truro (and Dallas). She didn't have a reinforced-concrete hairstyle: she didn't go in for sultry looks and fluttering eyelashes. She had a direct way with her. And she was seen by the Truro bourgeoisie as a whore, a gypsy, a threat to respectable marriage (even though she wasn't sleeping with Field). Yet she is *shown* as having integrity: she investigates Titus' blackmail of a building contractor to use Cuban labour, his engineering of a fire for insurance money, etc. While Constance, the socially-endorsed woman, is shown as a nasty piece of work, currently plotting with Titus to get rid of Lane – for ever. And *she's* the one that would make a Barbie doll look human.

But the central characters are not static. Field's new Senatorship is making him increasingly arrogant, and since she's been with him (3 episodes) Lane's hair is becoming concreter. So social qualities are not shown to reside just in individuals, but in *positions* of power, and stereotyped relationships. Most important, in the figure of Lane Ballou *Flamingo Road* connects what the world sees as a *sexual* threat, with a real threat to patriarchal power in society, and these aspects of her role are shown to fluctuate together. Moreover, for once sexuality is represented by *not* looking like a Barbie doll.

Does all this offer anything radical? *My* answer, which is yes, is echoed by a vast number of people – the Moral Majority of America. *Soap, Dallas* and *Flamingo Road* are all on their hit list, as programmes which undermine, not so much public institutions (Oil Corporations, Sheriffs) but The Family. It looks as if the Moral Majority has a real chance of success in banning these serials: I just hope people in America are less snobbish than the British and put up a fight for all three.

(City Limits, 1981)

CONSUMING PASSIONS

Body Heat *deals with a sexual attraction that is totally engulfing. For Ned Racine, his relationship with Matty Walker is paradoxically as liberating as it is ultimately destructive. Through it, Ned is put in touch with his deepest emotions, a wellspring of dark desires he never acknowledged in himself . . . writer-director Kasdan achieves a sensory visual beauty as the passion of his central characters hits the screen with torrential force. With the unflinching perceptions that have marked films as diverse yet unforgettable as* Double Indemnity, Sunset Boulevard, *or* The Maltese Falcon, *the corruption of these characters mirrors the corruption at the nerve centre of a system which makes a deity of success.*

Twenty pages of torrid prose like this characterize Warner's publicity handout for *Body Heat,* the first film directed by screenwriter Lawrence Kasdan (a Spielberg protégé who wrote *The Empire Strikes Back* and *Raiders of the Lost Ark).* It's one of the most striking in a recent wave of 'sexual passion' films – *Tess, Endless Love, Lady Chatterley's Lover, The Postman Always Rings Twice.* In a society which loves to proclaim its inclusion of the wild, exotic, and jungle-fresh on every street hoarding, this 'torrential force' of screen passion reveals a cinema industry which also delights in brandishing the 'danger' and 'dark forces' of its products. 'The Love Every Parent Fears' boasts the *Endless Love* poster. 'Carries Sexual Honesty to Dangerous Limits' thrills the blurb for the Frieda Lawrence character in the forthcoming *Priest of Love.*

Body Heat is in the mainstream of this hot flood: but like *The Postman* (a remake of the 1946 original), it also harks back to a certain strand of post-war cinema, with a plot based on the 1944 *Double Indemnity.* A sort of general nostalgia for this period is hovering around, with *Lili Marleen* or the earlier *New York, New York,* and also more generally in fashions and interior design. *Body Heat,* though set in the present, is nostalgic in its visual style – halfway between Raymond Chandler and a Dry Cane advert. But although it's seductive to watch, Kasdan's self-conscious attempt to evoke the 'film noir' movies of the '40s to '50s, and re-kindle their particular forms of passion, is beset with problems of the present.

'Film noir' gets its name from a visual style – an abundance of darkness and shadows, sharp contrasts of light and dark, night scenes and murky interiors rather than brightly-lit sets and daylight landscapes. But the term 'noir' also serves as a metaphor for aspects of content: a sense of moral uncertainty, difficulty in knowing the 'truth' (for the audience too, as the plots often hardly make sense) and in distinguishing between appearance and reality. The mood of frustration and bleakness in these films overpowers the righteous reassertion of law and traditional values in their endings. (The last word in this is *Kiss Me Deadly* where the solution to the plot and the search for meaning is the Pandora's 'box' that blows up the world). And most 'classic' films noirs are about crimes – usually resulting from the violent passions provoked by *femmes fatales* (like Gloria Grahame and Rita Hayworth) in illicit sexual relationships.

This core of violent passion, violent crime, and ultimate punishment, is focused on the figure of the woman who is totally desirable, but deeply feared. She embodies a threat to moral and social order: a defiance of, on the one hand, the law, through actual crimes (as in *They Live by Night*), and on the other hand, the structure of family relations. This may be through adultery (*Postman, Double Indemnity*), or simply through sexual relations which won't lead to marriage and family life, e.g. in prostitution, or an under-world setting (as with Gloria Grahame in *The Big Heat*). The way that breaking the bounds of marriage and family order always coincides with, or leads to, the *ultimate* crime (murder) can be seen in two ways. It connects sexual passion with violence, corruption, and the destruction of the lovers. (Marriage is rarely seen as sexual, it involves twin beds) It also connects the stability of the family unit with social law in a wider sense, the kind of laws which pass death sentences.

But the most striking aspect of the conflicts and ambi-guities in these films is that they confront *men,* in the form of *women.* The classic detective quest for the truth about *events* is transmuted into a search for the secret of the Sphinx, the 'true' nature of the sexual woman (which usually turns out to be treacherous – or at least, corrupt, as with Lauren Bacall in *The Big Sleep*). In *Double Indemnity,* after Barbara Stan-wyck and Fred MacMurray have murdered her husband to get his life insurance, she reveals that she was merely using MacMurray as a tool to get the money. This plot twist is echoed in *Body Heat,* but without the characteristic ambi-guity which the earlier film creates through Stanwyck's inability to fire a second shot at the man she claims not to love.

Ambiguity is a difficult quality to manufacture. Kasdan's deliberate 'film noir' is different from its models, because film noir was never a Hollywood 'genre' like the Western or Women's Weepie, deliberately produced by the studios for a particular audience. It was only 'recognized' retrospectively, when the term was coined by French critics; the films themselves involved confused and conflicting strands of feeling at a time when the social order was being profoundly changed. The period after the war was one of great disillusionment for many men returning home (a problem dealt with directly in the non-noir *The Best Years of Our Lives*). The society they had fought to defend was unable to welcome them back into a cosy niche – neither at work, nor at home, since women's war-time roles had changed, if not their social status, at least their aspirations. Film noir points to a telling preoccupation with the 'free' woman, the 'strong' woman, and particularly the woman who supports herself or has material ambitions – like *Mildred Pierce* (1945), a phenomenally determined single woman.

Significantly, the male heroes in film noir are always losers in some sense: in *Postman,* a bum who gets a job in a cafe, in *Double Indemnity* a hum-drum insurance salesman, in *The Big Heat,* a rather ordinary cop whose low income is stressed at the start. One function of film noir is to channel their frustration with routine jobs or lack of material success into the form of *sexual* ambitions. Social aspirations are latched onto illicit sex – and then firmly crushed in the name of 'morality'. Desire for Woman becomes merged with, and represents, desire for what society will not allow – which is why the former must be so violently punished.

In the melodramas of the '50s, punishment is replaced by voluntary renunciation. Twelve years on from *Double Indemnity,* Barbara Stanwyck and Fred MacMurray meet again in Douglas Sirk's *There's Always Tomorrow.* (What the film shows, of course, is that there isn't.) She, an old flame, meets the now married MacMurray, whose 'normal' domestic life is shown, depressingly realistically, as utterly lacking in passion, and completely dominated by children. But this time round, the tortured lovers suffer agonies of guilt, until Stanwyck renounces the affair (following a petition from MacMurray's dreadful offspring). The film ends with him in the toyshop where he works, watching a toy robot whose movements symbolize the mechanical emptiness of his own life, and the choice that has been made.

The '60s, however, brought an era of apparent liberation, and the beginning of the explicit portrayal of sex in 'non-porn' films. Shame was supposedly dispelled and sex 'freed' from fear and guilt. Just as more material goodies were available at this period, so was more sex. There seemed to be plenty to go round – a plenitude represented by The Orgy, or the multiple romps of *Tom Jones* and *Alfie*. Sexy women were still very much the prize – but now no man was punished for trying to win. The increase in upward social mobility linked up with this ability to *get* the beautiful woman, often of a higher social class (in *Billy Liar, Lucky Jim*), who had once seemed out of reach. But this general availability of sex, as it seemed, was not characterized by *passion:* sex was talked about as never before, de-mystified and in a sense contained, dealt with by being turned into something *healthy* – look, it's safe! It appeared to hold no threat.

But it did: the following decade saw the emergence of the *women's* liberation movement, challenging the roles that women had played hitherto in men's aspirations. There followed an interesting sequence of film trends: the women's films of the '70s (like *Girlfriends, Julia* and *The Turning Point),* the male angst/insecurity films that followed them *(10, Ordinary People, Starting Over)* and then the last two years' striking collection of violence-to-women films – *Dressed to Kill, Don't Answer the Phone, He Knows You're Alone,* etc., etc.

Where next? Back to passion, it seems, and a reaffirmation of the 'basic' desire between the sexes – which can easily be used to legitimize male domination. This year, steamy, sweaty *lust* is back in and nowhere more so than in *Body Heat.* Set in a heat wave in Florida, it follows the liaison of an unsuccessful young lawyer, Ned Racine, with Matty

Walker, the young and attractive wife of an older, wealthy businessman. They murder him to get his money, but it gradually becomes clear that Matty has planned to murder Ned too, and get away with the spoils. In these basics – and the style, mist replacing shadow as the element of murkiness – the movie does resemble its model, *Double Indemnity*. But *Body Heat*'s use of sexual passion has more to do with modern fears than with those of the '40s.

For all the film's hot sex scenes are given a particular slant by the way Ned's and Matty's first fuck is shown. The film presents Matty as totally 'seductive' in dress and behaviour, but having invited Ned to come back and see her wind chimes, she asks him to leave. Ned stands outside, staring at her – and we watch her too, through the glass windows of the house – standing still, a fetish object in her red skirt, 'inviting' through the very fact that she can be *seen*. Ned takes a garden chair and smashes the window; then as he reaches her she flings her arms round his neck. The next minute he puts his hand on her crotch and she says 'yes! yes!' and then they're on the floor, she begging 'now! now!'. It is as if *he* knows what she wants, even if *she* doesn't. It is precisely the notion of her *pleasure* which is used here to justify his acting against her will. All this seems to me like the thinking man's form of last year's sexual violence – but this time, they *like* it.

We later learn that Matty ensnared Ned deliberately. But we don't know it at the point when he smashes the window, and so the episode breaks from the original '40s scenarios, where the women never say no and mean yes: they are sexually complicit from the start.

Similarly in the earlier films the male characters were complicit in the evil that the woman symbolizes – a case of they've got it, even if she wears it. MacMurray is equally involved with Stanwyck in pushing her husband off a train, to claim the insurer's 'double indemnity' – twice as much money. But in *Body Heat*, Matty alone alters her husband's will to exclude his niece and gain twice as much – something which Ned opposes: 'Let's not get greedy'. Since when did anyone in film noir say 'let's not get greedy'? The film's anxiety to present Ned as innocent of *too much* crime, and the sense of his having been duped, not of having *participated*, seems to tie in with a post-women's movement feeling men have of being unfairly blamed for everything wrong in sexual relations. (Ned ends up in prison: Matty escapes to live in luxury.) Similarly, an anxiety about sex itself is perhaps revealed by the insistence on Ned's ability to fulfil Matty's 'insatiable' needs, in the pretty explicit – including oral and anal – sex scenes.

But despite the self-consciousness of the attempt, *Body Heat* does not achieve the sense of sexuality as a 'wellspring of dark desires' to which it lays claim. The lurking threat of destructive and mysterious sexual passion which haunts *Double Indemnity* and the '40s version of *Postman,* is very much at odds with the post-'60s idea that repression can be countered by *showing* sex, or talking about it. Those earlier movies made it painfully clear that any desire which transgressed the family set-up was to be suppressed, that only certain kinds of personal relationships are legitimized and protected by social law. The problem was not repression, but the whole organization of society. But the shift in representation since then has been an attempt to show more and more sex, while still holding it up as the great naughty secret. This contradiction becomes ridiculous in the new film noir – for how can a film simultaneously suggest that something is *out of bounds,* while flaunting its explicit *inclusion?* That crime was always punished in film noir indicates the power of society's laws. But how much easier to characterize problems of *op*pression as those of *re*pression – which can then be remedied merely by *showing.*

Who doesn't know the sense of impending doom that attends the merest flicker of an 'illicit' desire (let alone acting on it)? But how can *desire* be illicit? It depends on whether the *person* desired is of the same or opposite sex, married or unmarried – in other words, on social codes constructed and reinforced by agencies like the cinema. Yet it's desire itself which is blamed (unfairly!) for the trouble that ensues. Desires, in 'dark wellsprings' and 'corrupt nerve centres', always appear to be fatalistically doomed from the start. All they are really doomed to do is disrupt social conventions: but their depiction as inherently self-destructive turns them into useful channels for making all that is forbidden in society seem equally dangerous. Dedicated followers of passion should cast off, not shame, but the burden of carrying all the taboos of an oppressive system – of being the wild animal whose function is to show the tamer's skill.

(City Limits, 1982)

NO MORE THAN A MAN

10 was one of the outstandingly popular movies of the '70s. It is always difficult to pin down what makes a box-office hit, but perhaps the most successful films are those which strike on some contemporary problem or insecurity in the issues they raise, while resolving these issues in a satisfactory or unthreatening way. *10* seems to me to fit this formula very accurately, because it deals, fundamentally, with the male reaction to the women's movement and taps many current anxieties – about 'liberated' women, about impotence, ageing, masculinity, and, very obliquely, about homosexuality. These are also the concerns of, for example, Godard's *Slow Motion (Sauve Qui Peut – La Vie)* which, like *10*, hinges around two different versions of 'New Woman': the Male Psyche Under Threat theme has been running through both mainstream and 'Art' movies of the late '70s. The success of *10* is that it functions so as to defuse that threat, while still presenting it convincingly.

If a film is to tackle, for example, the male fears connected with the women's movement, it has to represent within it not only those fears but also their causes. This makes for contradictory sets of values, different possible meanings, different interpretations: in order to achieve its ultimately reassuring aim the film cannot crudely *impose* one interpretation or there would be nothing to overcome, no visible or felt threat to be dissolved. Out of the many different meanings and layers of discourse in the film, one set must finally dominate – but, as Gramsci says of the dominant or 'hegemonic' ideology, it must govern not by brute force and coercion but by a consent which has to be *won*. What *10* must do if it is to fulfil the function I have suggested, is both to represent liberated women and the threatened male ego, and yet to find ways within the film to undermine the former, and subtly bring the latter to a position of hegemony within the competing ideologies which it presents. I intend to focus on key points of conflict within the film to investigate which meanings are dominant and which are undercut, how this is achieved, and why.

Meanings are first circulated around a film before it even reaches the cinema, through publicity. As with many movies, *10* was sold to the public mainly on the basis of images which did not in fact exist anywhere in its narrative: the poster showed Dudley Moore and an almost-naked Bo Derek in an embrace on the sand. This doesn't even correspond to the fantasy sequence in the film where Dudley, sunbathing, daydreams of Bo Derek running towards him in her bathing suit. The image of Dudley and Bo embracing makes it look as if a large part of the film consists of them copulating on beaches, evoking a *fulfilment* to what, in the film, remains at the level of a wish – because in fact, when Dudley does get the chance to sleep with Bo, he becomes disillusioned with her and they never 'make it'.

The publicity, then, offers a consummation which the film, in a more complex way, frustrates, and indeed ends by suggesting is not worthwhile anyway. However, on a cruder but perhaps more crucial level, the publicity, and the whole aura of the film at the height of its success, centred quite simply on Bo Derek's figure – or, to be more precise, her bustline. For a brief period of our cultural history Bo Derek featured in the public eye in much the same vein as Erica

Roe, the woman who ran naked across a rugby pitch, and whose breasts became a major image in the popular imagination. The 'speech' which surrounded *10* was almost entirely about the size of Bo Derek's breasts – jokes about 'measurements' abounded and this bustline became the dominant image of the film. One memorable poster showed simply an enormous cleavage, in which a tiny Dudley Moore dangled, like a pendant on a chain – an economic portrayal of the famous breasts *and* male sensibility at the same time.

The way the film was represented *outside* the cinema through Bo Derek's bust and generally fantastic figure, implied that the relation of audience to film inside the cinema was a straightforwardly voyeuristic one, along the lines of male desire. The radio advertisement for *10* featured a couple arguing, the woman angry because her man had been to see *10* and wouldn't stop playing Ravel's 'Bolero' – the theme music from Bo Derek's one sex scene. In other words, the film was actually marketed by invoking a woman's jealousy at her husband or boyfriend fancying Bo Derek. This was reinforced by numerous women's magazine articles which presented Bo Derek as a threat: one item in *Company* showed a photo of her looking 'normal' in a dufflecoat, with the caption: 'For those of us who bitched whilst our menfolk lusted, it's comforting to know that even sex-symbols have their off-days . . .' and so on.

Now given that *10* is largely about *male* insecurity, it would seem that this image of it is misleading. Bo Derek is not even one of the main characters in the film; she is the object of Dudley Moore's fantasy but plays a relatively minor role. Yet although the publicity differs from the narrative content of the film, it does draw out its real sexual undercurrent – rather as graffiti often does, when the implicit sexuality in, say, a film poster, is brought to the surface by parts of the anatomy crudely added by kids. The whole area of film publicity is an interesting one in itself: many 'violence against women' films were picketed by feminists on the basis of their posters, which often depicted scenes of violence not actually found in the films, but indicative of the fantasies they evoked. An example is the poster for *The Shining,* a montage of two images, Shelley Duval screaming and Jack Nicholson with an axe, which were never juxtaposed in the movie. But, as we learn from dreams, images represent wishes, as much as facts.

From this angle the images and ideas surrounding *10* are uncannily accurate, since they are very close, not to the plot, but to the psyche of the male protagonist. A core of voyeuristic, infantile sexual wishes gets right outside the cinema, as it were, and takes over from the content of the film itself by evoking precisely Dudley Moore's ('George's') fantasies in a potential audience, weaned onto the film via Bo Derek's breasts.

The underlying *drive* of a film cannot be reduced to any particular part of the script. If the dialogue and plot of *10* were mapped out on paper, they would reveal a quite different story, dealing with issues like monogamy, sexual liberation, male chauvinism, insecurity, and ageing. But whatever the film appears to be when written out flat, when it actually comes alive in imagery it also functions on a quite different axis. Some images are more powerful than others, some film moments more crucial, some devices – gags, for example – more effective, and these *filmic* stresses create values and meanings which can cut across those of the dialogue; they can be both visually and emotionally more powerful than just 'talking'. Certain feelings are drawn out of the 'story' narrative and create, on a different level, a sort of psychological narrative, a 'sub-script' which is nowhere written or spoken but which carries the dominant meaning of the film – dominant because it works on the most unconscious level. All films have a certain quality which is like turning a head inside out; their movements and actions are powered by internal drives as much as external devices.

The main plot of *10* concerns George's (Dudley Moore's)

troubled relationship with his girlfriend Sam (Julie Andrews), an adult woman with her own career, and his growing fantasy about Jenny (Bo Derek) whom he glimpses on her wedding day and subsequently dreams of as a perfect virginal figure. After following her to Mexico he eventually meets Jenny in reality through saving her young husband from drowning. He has the chance to sleep with her but is disillusioned by her promiscuity, and ends up with Sam again. This is in many ways the classic Hollywood morality plot of fantasy pursued, fulfilled, and finally exploded, leading back to the 'home is best' type of finale with the return to the original lover/place/job etc. On this level the film deals with the issues of both women's liberation (as represented through the Julie Andrews figure) and sexual liberation (Bo Derek) and George's confrontations with each.

However, the 'psychological narrative' of the film is fundamentally the regression of George to an infantile state, until very near the end he is re-introduced to adulthood. My argument is that this level of the film, which works through visual organization, comedy, gags and timing, successfully undercuts the issues raised on the more 'serious' level, by providing the male character with a way out of every confrontation; since if he is represented psychologically as a child, all problems and conflicts become things which happen *to* him. This perfectly dramatizes the general male response to feminism and seems to have touched the raw nerve of a current strand of feeling, judging by the film's financial success.

We are first introduced to George's emotional problems as he chats with his gay colleague Hugh, who remarks, 'I could have analyzed you a lot better than that expensive shrink – the trouble is, you would have come out gay and I couldn't do that to Sam.' When George says 'I'll give her your love', Hugh tells him: 'Give her *yours*'. On the plot level, Sam, George and Hugh all move in the same world of professional musicians – Sam is a singer and George a composer. Right from the start there is an association of Sam with George's gay friend which forms an important part of the film's psychological movement. Because Hugh and Sam are so close, and Hugh always encourages George to stay with her, a certain suggestion of (male) homosexuality attaches itself to Sam; and since she does not fulfil a totally 'feminine' stereotype, George's relationship with her appears in some ways as not quite heterosexual enough. Even her name, abbreviated from 'Samantha', is that of a man. The theme of homosexuality is an oblique one in the film; it works not only through Hugh, but in the way that of the two women, one is set up as more 'masculine' (Julie Andrews) and one as 'feminine' (Bo Derek) so that in a certain sense George is offered, on this representational level, a choice between a homosexual and a heterosexual relationship. Yet because this choice is manifested as a choice between women, the film never really has to confront it as an overt issue – it is perhaps the most deeply buried sub-text of all. Nevertheless, it does seem to be one of the areas of anxiety for men that the film touches on, and has an important bearing on the portrayal of Sam.

The first key sequence in the film starts with George slotting a cassette into his car stereo, so that we hear Sam singing on the sound-track over shots of him curb-crawling in his car and eyeing up women on the sidewalk. The relation between sound and image here sets up the emotional space of the film, the arena in which its central drama is acted out. Her song – 'No more than a man' – stakes out the pitch:

> *'He's no more than a man*
> *Nothing special that you'd run to see*
> *He's a child to be sure*
> *At times insecure*
> *But he pleases me . . .*
> *He's a man, nothing more*

Sometimes clumsy and absent of mind
The mystery is what he sees in me . . .
Why should I ever doubt him
When I know all along
That the very best of men must roam.
Sure I get lonely without him
But a man, right or wrong,
The more you bind him,
the less you find him home . . .
He's no more than a man
Just a weaver of wishes and dreams
When he's shy, insecure,
He's a child, to be sure . . .'

At this point George crashes his car, having moved from cruising the first two girls he saw, to trailing Bo Derek whom he has glimpsed in her wedding car on the way to church. The steady continuation of Sam's song, despite all this, turns it into a kind of safety net for George. Even while he is chasing other women, there she is on the sound-track, full of understanding: 'He's a child' — and she is his mother. The whole persona of 'Cuddly Dudley', which comes from outside the film, contributes to this. On the other hand, Julie Andrews brings with her the persona of the Singing Nanny from *The Sound of Music*. There is no scope for her to be childish or threatened – he is enclosed by her voice as if in a playpen, within which he can do anything he wants and still be accepted. And he is placed as a child at just the moment when he starts to 'roam' – any threat *he* might pose to *Sam* through this is thus defused at the very start. This use of Sam's voice-over is repeated at several key points later, when a song from the musical she is acting in is used to accompany George's infantile wanderings. The number is titled 'I give my heart just to one man': although the plot-rationale makes the words merely part of Sam's *work*, at the rehearsal studio, in practice they serve to repeat the experience of the 'No more than a man' sequence, and to create in auditory form a sort of comfort-blanket for George while he follows his own whims.

His car crash – which he glides into as in a nightmare, just as Sam sings for the second time 'He's a child to be sure' – is the first in a string of gags and accidents which play a key role in turning George from an active adult into a passive infant. Kicking off from this crash, the mishaps which follow are: he is stung on the nose by a bee while hiding behind some flowers in the church, watching Jenny's wedding; he locks himself out of his house after an argument with Sam; he falls down a steep slope and cannot climb up to reach the phone in time to receive her call; he has several fillings at the dentist under a local anaesthetic which makes him dribble and spill coffee down himself in a restaurant while he's trying to pick up a woman; he then takes pain-killers and is incapable of speaking when the police are called to his house which he has 'broken into'; in this totally infantile state – dribbling, unable to talk or walk properly – he staggers next door to join in his neighbour's orgy, is seen at it by Sam thereby incurring her anger; arrives in Mexico (chasing Bo Derek) half-dead and has an impotent sexual encounter with a woman he meets there; the next morning he is unable even to walk across the beach, slipping on the sand and falling over.

Many of these scenes of physical incapacity can be seen as concerning impotence – as when he falls down the slope and, panting and gasping, can't *get up it* – the rearrangement of these three words gives the obvious sub-text to this and many other sequences, culminating in his actual sexual incapacity with the woman in Mexico. However, this meaning seems to me fairly obvious, as is the phallic significance of George's obsession with his telescope, and his neighbour's telescope, which is bigger. The most important thing about the telescope is that it revals the essentially voyeuristic nature of George's sexual activity (or non-activity). The film is full of sexual puns and phallic references, and since it sets out overtly to deal with male fears about ageing (it opens at George's fortieth birthday party) it is hardly surprising that impotence is a major theme.

However, I believe that the gags and incapacities of the male character have both a simpler and more basic function, which relates more to infantile regression than to phallic sexuality. For all the 'accidents' and gags come at moments when George is under threat from serious criticism posed as coming from a bossy or over-demanding woman. When any discussion of his behaviour arises – and this consists of a lot of the film's dialogue – it is instantly undercut through slips and accidents *which put the man in a passive position.* External physical things happen to him, just at the point when verbal criticisms are made of him, so that the two become psychologically fused. The panicky sense of frustration created by the timing of these incidents – like the classic example of reaching the phone just after it stops ringing – invites you to identify with the Dudley Moore character; and it is physical devices which create these nightmare feelings. The scene where he cannot walk across the sand in Mexico is taken almost straight out of those bad dreams when you want to run but can't – when you have no control over your actions. Through such means George is turned into somebody passive, to whom things happen. This seems to me to represent very clearly the man-under-pressure feeling at the heart of the film.

Of course, these gags are a reminder that Blake Edwards also directed the 'Pink Panther' films. The gag is both a theatrical and a filmic device that relies on timing and comic acting. But its function in *10* is quite particular, and its timing is crucial not just for the internal functioning of the gag, but its function within the narrative. The initial car crash takes place because Dudley is watching Bo Derek and not the road. Yet the physical sensation of a car crash is of something happening *to* you, and instantly, something caused by George's own actions is felt, *physically*, as an act of fate, in which he is the victim.

The next major 'accident' comes, conveniently, after he has had an argument with Sam and is meant to apologize. Whenever anything of substance happens within this relationship, George is quickly put into the position where he 'couldn't help it'. He becomes increasingly powerless as the issues of his commitment, sexuality, and male chauvinism become more clearly defined. If this was an Art Movie about Modern Relationships, we might take more notice of this aspect of the film and those parts of the dialogue where sexism is discussed in detail. But every time these issues are raised, the film slips a gear and the narrative is by-passed, not by an opposing *idea,* but by a switch to a different level entirely, one of physical effects. These create a current of feeling – whether funny, painful or downright frustrating – which pulls everything else along with it. The accelerating pile-up of incapacitation – the dentist visit, his dribbling, being unable to speak, etc. – not only returns George to the literal state of an infant, but puts the audience in a position to share his sensation of incapacity and frustration through basic film mechanisms: for example the simple device of intercutting between the ringing telephone and George scrambling up the slope.

Having regressed to a point of total motor discoordination, George staggers half-clothed and inarticulate to join the orgy next door which he has hitherto merely envied through his telescope. This orgy, the mecca of his infantilism, is like an enactment of polymorphous, undifferentiated sexuality; the true site of George's regression. He has, in fact, moved *backwards* through almost classically Freudian phases of sexual development. It is interesting that the dentist who does George's teeth, thereby incapacitating him for much of the film, is Jenny's *father*. It is worth noting that Freud interprets fears of losing teeth and dentist nightmares as representing the fear of castration. The white-coated dentist wielding a large drill is a very powerful image of bodily threat and this interpretation would seem justified given, first, George's obsession with his telescope and other phallic objects, and second, the dentist being Jenny's father – which puts him in the classic place of the castrating father. The fact that George's entire vision of Jenny is based on seeing her getting *married* would also seem to fit in with this particular psychological schema.

However, after the dentist's anaesthetic George seems to move into a sort of pre-oedipal phase of complete babydom and unbounded sexual experience. When he staggers off to join the orgy, completely out of his head, he is returned to a morass of physical one-ness with other bodies. The anaesthetic and the drugs he has taken put him in a symbiotic relationship to the outer world – literally, since he cannot feel the boundaries of his own body. So when Sam finally breaks into his house and sees him, through the telescope, at the orgy next door, her anger doesn't *feel* like a consequence of his *activity,* it feels like one more thing happening to him. The whole scene has the nature of another 'accident' (a bit like being told off for wetting yourself – another connotation of the word). This is reinforced by the fact that as he looks through his neighbour's telescope and sees her seeing *him,* it swings round and hits him on the head. Even the telescope, the means of his voyeurism, is switched from being his *instrument* into something which acts *on* him. As he is struck by it, we identify with him and not – unless we make an effort – with Sam (who is understandably fed up). Similarly, when George is tumbling down the slope in the telephone sequence, we become so physically bound up with his flounderings that we forget the reason behind the whole scene, which is that he owes Sam an apology. This constant turning round of his activity into passivity perfectly reproduces the sensation of being threatened which men seem to experience in relation to women.

The saga of regression peaks at the beginning of George's

stay in Mexico, when, while he's floundering on the beach, Jenny's hunky husband actually kicks sand in his face – the nadir of weediness. But as he lies on the sand fantasizing about Jenny, the plot suddenly switches from fantasy to reality and George realizes that the young husband is drifting out to sea in his dinghy. There then follows a kind of triumph of the superego, for instead of letting the man who stands between himself and Jenny float out of the way, George quickly gets a boat and goes out to save him. It is very like the classic resolution to the Oedipus complex: morality dictates that you cannot kill Daddy in order to have Mummy (and her breasts), and Freud claims that on acceptance of this taboo rests the male sense of justice and morality. From the point where he saves Jenny's husband, George suddenly grows up and commands respect: his *professional* status is stressed for the first time, as he performs that evening at the piano – and he becomes, finally, morally *superior* to Jenny, whom he has been grovelling after throughout the rest of the film. Saving her husband gives him access to a higher morality and he 'grows up' just in time to undermine *her* position, having already, from a different angle, undermined Sam's.

This sudden switch is essential if George is to combat successfully *both* the women in the plot, or rather, the ideology which each stands for. For the *dialogue* in scenes with Julie Andrews and Bo Derek gives the two women very strong roles, arguing for, respectively, women's liberation and sexual liberation. The women are set up as opposites throughout the film, partly through its structure – for example, George following Jenny while Sam is singing her song. However, it is mainly felt because George *sees* them as opposites. (This echoes the *Company* article about 'our menfolk lusting after Bo Derek' – we are supposed to identify with Sam.) But there is nothing at all in what either of the two women *says* which indicates that they have opposite ideas. Taken together, their speeches add up to a well-founded argument for women to be taken seriously, sexually and in every other respect – and moreover, for the idea that one is responsible for one's own happiness, a concept which is way beyond George.

Two key scenes, one with each woman, are worth examining in detail for some clues as to how these feminist ideas, which must appear very explicit in the written script of the film, are undercut and ultimately put down in ways which reinforce precisely the sexism and moralism they are attacking. The first is a brilliant argument scene between Dudley Moore and Julie Andrews, which takes place at night when Sam wants to go to bed and George is busy peering through his telescope at the orgy next door.

George: 'That son-of-a-bitch across the way's got a bigger telescope than we have.'

Sam: 'Not *we* have, *you* have – I don't keep peering through somebody else's windows to get my jollies – you're a dirty old man George and so's your friend.'

George: 'He's not my friend –'

Sam: 'Well he should be, you must know him intimately by now.'

George: 'I don't watch him, I watch his broads – he's got a hell of a stable over there.'

Sam: 'Then he must be pretty good in the sack, huh?'

George: 'What's that got to do with it?'

Sam: 'Well, unless he's using some new, remote-control screwing device, how can you keep from watching him too?'

George: 'I concentrate on the broads.'

Sam: 'Well he's around, isn't he?'

George: 'What are you getting so het up for?'

Sam: 'Well, have you got the time, or do you want to wait 'til after the late show?'

Despite his preoccupation with watching women, George is

paradoxically portrayed as under unreasonable pressure from his girlfriend's sexual demands. On paper, she has already, in this scene, criticized his voyeurism, and made a sexual invitation – something which is connected with her *bossiness* in the way the whole sequence is constructed.

Sam: 'First, I am getting a little fed up at sexually emancipated women being referred to as broads. Second, I think a telescope aimed at anything other than the stars is an invasion of privacy, and qualifies the viewer as a peeping tom and there's a very good law against that.
Third, the first two really wouldn't bother me a bit if you'd stop watching so goddam much television and pay a little more attention to your bedroom guests – this guest in particular.
Now – do you want to argue or do you want to make love?'

Sam not only makes her own sexual demands but, far from 'bitching' or showing jealously of the women George ogles, she demands that he stop referring to them as 'broads'. She certainly does not act like a mother: but this is the role she ends up being placed in through George's interpretation of her criticisms as 'telling him off'. There follows a long argument about whether or not the term 'broad' is derogatory:

George: 'Define broad.'
Sam: 'Your definition or mine?'
George: 'Well I know yours.'
Sam: 'A girl who screws around a lot.'
George: 'A hooker.'
Sam: 'A hooker's a hooker – the fact that they both spread their legs doesn't make the terminology exchangeable.'
George: 'What's the difference?'

Sam: 'A hooker sells it.'

George: 'And so does a broad. The only difference is a hooker makes the price going in.'

Sam: 'Ah – so by definition, the broad is less virtuous than the hooker.'

George: 'As far as I'm concerned, virtue's got absolutely nothing to do with it.'

Sam: 'As far as you're concerned, or any man for that matter, virtue has everything to do with it.'

George: 'Listen, I just said "broad".'

Sam: 'Are you really trying to tell me that "broad" is not a term used by men to describe women in a disparaging fashion?' . . .

And so it goes on, until they turn to the dictionary for a definition and, sure enough, find the word 'broad' listed as derogatory. After she has won her point, and George is sulking, Sam finally says, 'You know what's the matter with you, George –'

'Oh, male chauvinist pig, yes.'

'Besides that. You're gutless. You're afraid to admit that you blew it and lose like a man.'

'I wouldn't mind losing like a man, if you weren't so damned determined to win like one.'

Written out as dialogue this is a very hard scene, and it contains a serious statement of anti-sexism: Sam wins the argument and George is shown up as the male chauvinist he is. But in the film itself, this level is subsumed within the other dimension of George's passivity. During this sequence, Sam puts on her glasses for the first time, and at the moment when she reads the dictionary she looks like a caricature of the bookish schoolmarm, so that at just the point where he makes his complaint about her winning 'like a man', the *image* sets her up in an 'unfeminine' and 'male' role. She is dominant in the frame throughout the entire sequence, particularly at its end, where she is much higher and is looking down on him. George, on the other hand, has an enormous, bright red bee sting on his nose from the previous sequence, which makes him a figure of both humour and sympathy. It provides a let-out – it is impossible to take the scene too seriously when he has this clownish, bulbous nose that makes his every remark at once comic and pathetic. The combination of Sam as the hard-headed woman in glasses dominating as she reads the dictionary, and poor old George, a walking image of suffering with his giant bee sting (though this 'accident' was caused by his own voyeurism) – makes it almost seem as if it is *she* who has put George in this painful and vulnerable position. Whenever she says anything serious to him he always happens to be conveniently injured, or fall over, or to be victimized through some physical device that counteracts the dialogue.

Sam's speech in this scene, if taken seriously, would provide a perfect analysis of George's fantasy about Jenny, hingeing as it does on an ideal of 'virtue' (glimpsed in her bridal veil) – and moreover would agree with most of what *she* says to George in the Mexico sequence. Yet Sam and Jenny are psychologically posed as opposites, in what is an arbitrary but very typical way; not just within films and representations generally, but in ideas about women in real life. The idea that he has options places the male hero in a classically secure position.

After George has saved her husband (who is taken to hospital) Jenny invites him to go to bed with her, a feat which she organizes to the accompaniment of Ravel's 'Bolero'. However, when he asks her why she is making love with him, and she answers, 'Why not?', George's ideal of the fresh and innocent bride is shattered and he starts telling her off for having an affair with the man who saved her husband's life – though this is partly pride on his part:

George: 'I thought maybe you thought I was something more than just a casual lay.'
Jenny: 'Why did you think that?'

George: 'Oh great, thank you. – Because I thought you were something different – something special.'

Jenny: 'Yes, as far as I'm concerned I'm very special. And if I feel like sleeping with someone I do it because I want to, I enjoy it, it pleases me.'

George: 'Jolly good! But there's more to life than turning
(furious) on and screwing to Ravel's "Bolero".'

Jenny: 'Sure there is, but there's nothing *wrong* with turning on and screwing to Ravel's "Bolero".'

Then they argue about whether or not Jenny has a 'problem', since George thinks there's something wrong with her for being so willing to have sex with him.

As in the earlier argument with Sam, the text here offers a serious criticism of George's mores; in this case, of the moralistic fantasy in which he expects Jenny to be 'pure', and his disappointment at her unromantic motives. It would be possible to merge Sam's more consciously feminist speech, and Jenny's defense of sexual liberation, into one coherent critique of George's behaviour; indeed both speeches show how George's *idealization* of Jenny is merely the flip-side of his preoccupation with 'broads' and is an integral part of his voyeurism and fantasy life – in short, of his sexism. But the two scenes are played as total opposites. In the first George is the poor beleaguered male, being moralized *to,* and already retreating into his baby-boy role. By the time the Jenny sequence arrives, *he* is the moralist, *he* is grown-up. He has gained in stature in every way: through the saving of the husband, his long regression has been suddenly reversed, and many little details in the scene reinforce his supposed maturity in contrast with Jenny, who is made particularly vacuous. So just as the first major critique of George's sexism is undercut by *his* comic silliness, here, what might have been a powerful critique of his sexual double standards is undercut by making *Jenny* so silly. She squeals too much and jumps childishly on the bed; beads swinging from her hair get in the way of their embrace; she is obsessive about turning the record of 'Bolero' back to the beginning after every interruption – altogether, she is presented as slightly 'over the top'. If a woman who believed in sexual freedom had been pictured as not *quite* so silly, the scene would have been more ambiguous. However, since the two women have been set up as alternatives, it is reassuring to believe that George's fantasy has been *justifiably* exploded, because this allows him to go back to Sam. In reality, though, his change of heart derives not from a sudden re-discovery of Sam, but from his disillusion when Jenny turns out not to be the virgin bride he had imagined – a fantasy which Sam would have been the first to criticize.

Both women in the film are strong and articulate and both are sexually active and demanding. Neither acts as George would like, or as he expects. Their opposition in the movie reveals more about male fantasy than about these characters themselves. At the beginning Sam is the boring, nagging old mother-figure; George would rather watch TV than make love with her. At this point Jenny is attractive, exciting, desirable. Towards the end they are divided differently: Jenny is careless, unromantic, a-moral, Sam in contrast appears loving and affectionate and serious. The way they are played off against each other is always via the pivot of the man – illustrating yet again the centrality of the *male* psyche to the workings of the film.

This brings us back to the original question of dominant meanings. The sections of dialogue that I have quoted in detail reveal how the film contains within it a powerful and coherent critique of its own fundamental drive, in the words of the women characters, but uses what one might term below the belt tactics to defuse and undercut these critiques. Of course it is possible to interpret the film in different ways; on first viewing I was very surprised, given the nature of its publicity, by the strength of its 'feminist' dialogue. But ultimately this is an interpretation which can only be made by wilfully going against the grain of the movie, because the slapstick and physical effects force you to identify *physically* with George in his regression and mishaps.

Film is a physical medium: it has the capacity for actual physical effects. If you put a camera on a roller coaster or fast car, you can create the sensation in an audience of *being* in a roller coaster or fast car. It is possible to make people feel actually sea-sick in this way. This is an effect quite peculiar to film, and one which seems to have been neglected in film theory, although much has been written about visual point-of-view. But this is not the same thing. When we cut from George sliding around on the slope to the ringing telephone and back again, we are not placed *visually* in George's position, we *watch* him – but a sensation of frustration is created, and this does place us in precisely his *physical/emotional* position. Film theory has also made much of audience identification with male heroes as initiators of the action. What has been less observed is the capacity for identification in *passivity*. We do not feel that George creates the action – we feel he is a *victim* of events, and again, this feeling is very similar to that evoked by watching a film, when we are, literally, at the mercy of its movement and pace – the movie happens to us. This is one of the features films share with dreams. We all invent our dreams – we create the events that happen in them, they are fuelled by *our* wishes. Yet they seem to happen *to* us, they just 'come to us'. We experience them as if someone else has written the script. And this is very much how George in *10* experiences his own life.

This lets him off the hook in the face of feminism – which is where the film functions so powerfully in allaying contemporary male fears. What could be more reassuring than to find, first, that George is justified in lusting after Bo Derek because his girlfriend is such a cross old stick, second, that tubby, ageing George can *have* the sexy young girl he is after, and third, that she isn't worth having anyway? Most men can conveniently skip the middle stage and relax in the knowledge that, while you could of course have it if you wanted, it isn't really worth it.*

There might be more grounds for a 'feminist' interpretation of *10* – given that its main female figure, Sam, is explicitly feminist – if it were not for the very crude, in fact distressing sexism that slips out in the treatment of some of the minor female characters. It is often in odd corners like these that a film's fundamental ideology is revealed because, as with jokes, they seem trivial, but they are also more 'off guard' moments.

One of these characters is the old woman servant at the vicar's house where George goes in his quest for Jenny; she is almost blind, farts, falls over, and is made fun of in a peculiarly upsetting way. Another is the dentist's assistant, who is presented as a typical 'dumb blonde'. Then there are the women at the orgy – George's 'broads' – who are throughout the object of voyeuristic titillation not only for George but for the audience. Finally, there is the woman who sleeps with George in Mexico, a relatively important figure in terms of the film's theme of ageing. When George is impotent on going to bed with her, this is presented as an effect of her 'unattractiveness', and she has some key lines when, sitting morosely at the bar, she ponders the fact that men grow old and look distinguished, while women grow old and unattractive. 'What's fair about that?' she asks – and the barman agrees that nothing's fair about it. The supposed truth of the idea is not questioned. Although this seems like a meaningful little moment in the film, it is quite unnecessary – after all, the woman could have been made more attractive – the film has *made* her unglamorous and pitiable. But it is the old dream-theme again – it just 'happens' to be

---

*A re-run of many of these themes is found in the Dudley Moore film *Unfaithfully Yours* (1984), where his obsessive jealousy of his beautiful and much younger wife, resulting in a plot to kill her, turns out to be unfounded – implying that the only thing wrong in his behaviour was that it was based on an *error* – not on grossly possessive, violent sexism. As in *10*, this film allows male sexual fears to be *acted out*, but reassuringly shows them to be ultimately unfounded.

like that, the older woman just 'is' unattractive, and she just does 'make' George impotent.

Brecht once said of theatre, that people ought not to be represented as if they could only act one way in any given situation: they could act differently. Films tend to make you feel that the events and people pictured could *only* have been as they are shown – and this is not only true of Hollywood films, it applies just as much to most of the 'avant-garde'. The dreamer is presented with his or her own thoughts and desires as if they were not her/his own – a phenomenon externalized in Greek literature where 'The Gods' are the initiators of actions and emotions that 'happen to' people: which is why there is a god or goddess for just about every named emotion. In most films, which centre on the male psyche, there is, not a god, but a goddess for every emotion, or rather a woman for every shifting fear or desire of the male ego. I have tried to show how in *10* the female characters do in fact have a potentially radical discourse independent of the male 'hero' – yet their roles in his own dualist fantasy are stronger, and over-ride such potential. Ultimately, the audience has no choice but to endorse the sentiments of the theme tune. Yes, he's a little wayward and absent, he behaves badly, but he's a child at heart – often irritating, insufferably sexist, he's *'No more than a Man':* which seems to explain everything. How could he be different? But what it explains, of course, is the film itself.

(Based on a talk given at the National Film Theatre, London 1982.)

DO NOTHING

Today I walk along this lonely street
Trying to find, find a future
New pair of shoes are on my feet
'Cos fashion is, my only culture

Nothing ever change
Oh no . . .
Nothing ever change

People say to me just be yourself
It makes no sense to follow fashion
How can I be anybody else
I don't try, I've got no reason

Nothing ever change
Oh no . . .
Nothing ever change

I'm just living in a life without meaning
I walk and walk, do nothing
I'm just living in a life without meaning
I talk and talk, say nothing

Nothing ever change
Oh no . . .
Nothing ever change

Walk along the same old lonely street
Still trying to find, find a reason
Policeman come and smack me in the teeth
I don't complain, it's not my function

Nothing ever change
Oh no . . .
Nothing ever change

They're just living in a life without meaning
I walk and walk, do nothing
They're just living in a life without meaning
They talk and talk, say nothing

I'm just living in a life without meaning
I walk and walk, I'm dreaming . . .

Lynval Golding, *'Do Nothing'*
(for The Specials)

BELONGING TO US

What I would like to share with you for a few final moments is a vision of the things that matter most to me . . . I offer the certainty of liberty, and the chance of property ownership. *And not just a chance; that people should be able to own their own home is deep at the heart of Conservative philosophy. What earthly use is it that families should have a millionth share of some nationalized industry? How much more important to have something they can own and that can be passed on to their children. Never mind about public ownership – in practice that gives nobody anything. What I'm offering is* personal *ownership . . . property brings with it security and independence.*
(Margaret Thatcher, election broadcast)

In a world of fear, people cling desperately to their own possessions. In a world of poverty, people think first about their own children and their futures. In a world of insecurities, Home becomes more than ever a symbol of yearned-for security. Home, whatever it means to each of us, has become the most *publicly* wielded image of *private* security – a security apparently to be bought, to be owned, to be mortgaged. Mrs Thatcher, setting up society – 'public' – and individuals – 'personal' – in opposition, paints a picture that is actually becoming true. The society we live in does feel more like an enemy every day. *'Social* security' is now inadequate to provide just that. The tragedy is, that as this right-wing government makes ordinary life harder and harder, it creates the social conditions for precisely the individual fears and anxieties which fuel its support.

The depression I feel is not just my own. If we believe that our identities are formed in society, then this Tory determination to pull out, like a wilful child, every separate strand from the fabric of our social life is not just 'reactionary' but *painful,* bulldozing the ground on which we grew. The sense of the Welfare State is one of the earliest things I can remember, the delicious Clinic Orange Juice that was quite unlike 'bought', the equally foul free Cod-Liver Oil, the reverence with which my father spoke of Nye Bevan, an idea that the world was supposed to get better.

These feelings are Home to me, and without them I feel like an alien. Home is not property, it is belonging somewhere. Outside, children are playing on the shared pavements, beyond the emotional violence of particular families. Who owns the view from my window? What makes a street more homely than a house, a Council Estate safer than Real Estate, the whole of London more personal than a back garden?

I remember the title of a book on my parents' shelves, ingrained in my mind for twenty-five years: 'London Belongs To Me'. This exciting phrase always seemed both intimate and radical. As a recent *City Limits* feature showed, London belongs, mainly, to the Duke of Westminster, 'God', and the Queen. But it is also mine, and everyone's who lives in it, works in it and loves it, and it is this sense of belonging as an active relation which Tory individualism has frozen into 'belongings' – things owned.

Property *is,* as Mrs Thatcher says, deep at the heart of the Tories' (capitalist) philosophy – selling us back individually the very 'place' they destroy socially. Which is why, as socialists, we will have not just to fight, but to hold on to every glimmer of that other, intangible and priceless sense of 'belonging' if this society is to become a place to feel at home in again.

(*City Limits,* 1983)

URBAN SPACEMAN

A vodka advertisement in the London underground shows a cartoon man and woman with little headphones over their ears and little cassette-players over their shoulders. One of them holds up a card which asks, 'Your place or mine?' – so incapable are they of communicating in any other way. The walkman has become a familiar image of modern urban life, creating troops of sleep-walking space-creatures, who seem to feel themselves invisible because they imagine that what they're listening to is inaudible. It rarely is: nothing is more irritating than the gnats' orchestra which so frequently assails the fellow-passenger of an oblivious walk-person – sounding, literally, like a flea in your ear. Although disconcertingly insubstantial, this phantom music has all the piercing insistency of a digital watch alarm; it is your request to the headphoned one to turn it down that cannot be heard. The argument that the walkman protects the *public* from hearing one person's sounds, is back-to-front: it is the walk-person who is protected from the outside world, for whether or not their music is audible they are shut off as if by a spell.

The walkman is a vivid symbol of our time. It provides a concrete image of alienation, suggesting an implicit hostility to, and isolation from, the environment in which it is worn.

Yet it also embodies the underlying values of precisely the society which produces that alienation – those principles which are the lynch-pin of Thatcherite Britain: individualism, privatization and 'choice'. The walkman is primarily a way of escaping from a *shared* experience or environment. It produces a privatized sound, in the public domain; a weapon of the individual against the communal. It attempts to negate *chance:* you never know what you are going to hear on a bus or in the streets, but the walk-person is buffered against the unexpected – an apparent triumph of individual control over social spontaneity. Of course, *what* the walk-person controls is very limited; they can only affect their *own* environment, and although this may make the individual *feel* active (or even rebellious) in social terms they are absolutely passive. The wearer of a walkman states that they expect to make no input into the social arena, no speech, no reaction, no intervention. Their own body is the extent of their domain. The turning of desire for control inwards towards the body has been a much more general phenomenon of recent years; as if one's muscles or jogging record were all that one *could* improve in this world. But while everyone listens to whatever they want within their 'private' domestic space, the peculiarity of the walkman is that it turns the inside of the head into a mobile home – rather like the building society image of the couple who, instead of an umbrella, carry a tiled roof over their heads (to protect them against hazards created by the same system that provides their mortgage).

This interpretation of the walkman may seem extreme, but only because first, we have become accustomed to the privatization of social space, and second, we have come to regard sound as secondary to sight – a sort of accompaniment to a life which appears as essentially visual. Imagine people walking round the streets with little TVs strapped in front of their eyes, because they would rather watch a favourite film or programme than see where they were going, and what was going on around them. (It could be argued that this would be too dangerous – but how about the thousands of suicidal cyclists who prefer taped music to their own safety?) This bizarre idea is no more extreme in principle than the walkman. In the visual media there has already been a move from the social setting of the cinema, to the privacy of the TV set in the living-room, and personalized mobile viewing would be the logical next step. In all media, the technology of this century has been directed towards a shift, first from the social to the private – from concert to record-player – and then of the private *into* the social – exemplified by the walkman, which, paradoxically, allows someone to listen to a recording of a public concert, in public, completely privately.

The contemporary antithesis to the walkman is perhaps the appropriately named ghetto-blaster. Music in the street or played too loud indoors *can* be extremely anti-social – although at least its perpetrators can hear you when you come and tell them to shut up. Yet in its current use, the ghetto-blaster stands for a shared experience, a communal event. Outdoors, ghetto-blasters are seldom used by only their individual owners, but rather act as the focal point for a group, something to gather around. In urban life 'the streets' stand for shared existence, a common understanding, a place that is owned by no-one and used by everyone. The traditional custom of giving people the 'freedom of the city' has a meaning which can be appropriated for ourselves today. There *is* a kind of freedom about *chance* encounters, which is why conversations and arguments in buses and bus-queues are often so much livelier than those of the wittiest dinner party. Help is also easy to come by on urban streets, whether with a burst shopping bag or a road accident.

It would be a great romanticization not to admit that all these social places can also hold danger, abuse, violence. But, in both its good and bad aspects, urban space is like the physical medium of society itself. The prevailing ideology sees society as simply a mathematical sum of its individual parts, a collection of private interests. Yet social life demonstrates the transformation of quantity into quality: it has something extra, over and above the characteristics of its members in isolation. That 'something extra' is unpredictable, unfixed, and resides in interaction. It would be a victory for the same forces that have slashed public transport and privatized British Telecom, if the day were to come when everyone walked the street in headphones.

(1984)

NUCLEAR FAMILY? NO THANKS

There is a familiar car sticker which pictures a smiling sun wreathed by the words 'Nuclear Power? No thanks'. From the tone of the answer, one might think the question posed had been 'More sherry?' rather than 'Destruction of life on earth?'. But the multinational commercial interests and the governments that serve them are unlikely to listen to this genteel reply because they never asked a question in the first place. The persistent faith of the middle-class in politeness is perversely inappropriate in a world which it governs largely through the ruthless pursuit of political and economic power. The car sticker, with its cheerily inane smile, makes the mistake of suggesting that a choice has been offered. It hasn't.

I should say at the outset that I am totally opposed to nuclear power and nuclear weapons – their danger is not in question. What I do want to query are some of the ideological strategies of the anti-nuclear movement. The campaigns against nuclear fuels and nuclear missiles are extremely important, and are impressive in a great many ways. Yet in a few aspects they involve assumptions that are in direct conflict with either a feminist or a socialist understanding. There is an emphasis on motherhood, the family, woman as nature and as provider – exactly the myths about femininity that the women's movement has tried to question. There is also an emphasis on the individual and personal – related, as always, to the family/parenthood domain – rather than on the social; which is perhaps why this particular political arena is especially appealing to the middle-classes.

In the same way that it is difficult to criticize one's mother, because she is always right, so it is very difficult for feminists to criticize the Greenham Common campaign, because it seems haloed with that Women's Righteousness which has traditionally gone hand in hand with our oppression. Motherhood is always good, whether in Nazi propaganda or Persil ads; it lends a 'natural goodness' to the notion of 'Women Against the Bomb'. In the patriarchal values of modern capitalism, Woman is the great provider of nature and nurture: 'There are two men in my life, to one I am a mother, to the other I'm a wife. And I give them both the best. With Natural Shredded Wheat.' Is that ideology really so different from this: 'I think that most women are really in touch with what life is about. You can't even contemplate having a child without considering the value of that life and the struggle people have bringing up children, putting in all those hours and hours of caring. A lot of women do that not even with children, but with the home, making a wonderful place for people to get by day-to-day living. You just can't contemplate that being destroyed . . .'*

As if it is simply the *home,* with all the 'hours and hours' of caring (and dusting and polishing) one has put into it, that women can't bear to see destroyed! What about our society, cities, hospitals, libraries, histories, cultures, all the human achievements of thousands of years of social life? A social life that is women's work, as much as men's. We have been *taught* to think of our own families, homes and children as

*Quoted in *Greenham Women Everywhere,* by Alice Cook and Gwyn Kirk. All further quotes below are taken from different women's accounts collected in this book. They are not quotations from the authors.

the extent of our political concern and the sole focus for our 'caring'. On December 12th 1982 a demonstration took place in which the perimeter fence of the Greenham airbase was hung with symbols of whatever people most valued; it ended up covered in family snaps, wedding photos, anniversary cards (even some pictures of the Pope!) plus nappies, teddy bears and other symbols of childhood. Although the decoration of the fence was a powerful symbolic act in itself, the most persistent image was that of the nuclear family; and in a sense *what* the fence came to symbolize was the potential destruction of bourgeois family life by the bomb.

For women to identify with this image of the family seems like a giant step back from the politics of the women's liberation movement. Of course, the great irony about this notion of women as *inherently* more 'caring' than men (rather than as *conditioned* to be so) is that the most right-wing and militaristic Prime Minister we have had since the last war is a woman. But it can be argued that, like Lady Macbeth, she is going against her 'nature'. Women are supposedly the same the world over: 'Women can identify with women of Russia and Eastern bloc countries. We're just the same. A woman in Russia is the same as myself – the same emotions, leading the same sort of life. In no way will I be a part of anything that will murder her.' While one can admire the internationalist sentiment of this, the idea of women being fundamentally the same throughout the world can act as a cover for real differences in and between societies. The idea that women's 'Nature' can be mobilized against the nuclear threat also tends to naturalize that threat; as if men naturally created nuclear weapons and women naturally opposed them. This glosses over the actual system of political and economic power which profits from the production of nuclear weapons. But many of those who oppose nuclear weapons do not, in other ways, oppose that system. Nuclear war is undiscriminating: it is fatal for

oppressor and oppressed alike. Yet it is the relations of social oppression already in existence which have produced nuclear weapons, and which must therefore be attacked by any opponent of those weapons. The basic fear of destruction for oneself and one's children has no more political meaning in itself than the fear of being run over. Not that this is by any means the prerogative of women: in his book *The Dialectics of Disaster – a Preface to Hope* Ronald Aronson says, with wounded pride: 'As a father, I cannot be a father, because my girls are not safe and I cannot make them safe.' This ideology *limits* the notion of caring to parenthood; conveniently, since if the values of 'caring' were taken beyond the family they would involve fighting for far more radical changes in society.

There is one sense in which the idea of 'caring' *is* taken beyond the individual. But it is taken not into the realm of the *social,* but of the *natural.* Women apparently have more concern for the planet than men; and a more symbiotic relation to nature. 'You are a spring and if you copy this letter and send it to ten other women, who then do the same, we will become rivers that will flow together on December 12th and become an ocean of women's energy.' (Leaflet). There is a semi-mystical relation between women and ecology which again hinges upon the role of women as mothers – 'As women we wish to protect all life on this planet' (another leaflet) – and suggests some primeval state of unity between women and the earth – 'men have taken our property rights in the earth'. The ecology movement is very important, but where it combines with this particular kind of 'feminism' the result is a set of ideas uncomfortably close to the ideology of patriarchy itself. 'Babies against the Bomb', for example, draws on a sentimentality and notion of 'human nature' which are on the same level as 'human interest' items in the popular press. It turns a political movement into a natural one, in the same way that taking action 'because' one is a woman undermines the political deliberation of that action. Individual babies even have their own slogans: 'Amy against the Bomb' proclaimed the placard on the pram of a few-weeks-old baby on one demonstration. If babies, who do not make decisions, are against the bomb, what does this imply about the movement as a whole? Surely we should claim social consciousness, not natural instincts, as the basis of concerted action – especially since women have traditionally been regarded as instinctive bundles of emotion rather than as thinking, arguing people.

Unfortunately this traditional image has been the one most courted by some women in the peace movement, not only as the basis for their action but in its method as well. There is the wool weaving: 'We spin and thread ourselves together as women for this day . . .' reads one leaflet, and another: 'How will you do the action? Weave wool, link arms, sing . . .'. This can provide a powerful image – the whole point of such action is that woven wool *cannot* stop bombs, it is a symbol of *peace*. Yet sometimes it is treated as if it really had a mystical effect. One leaflet describes a 'full moon festival' at Greenham where 'a rainbow dragon will be *born* by joining the creative work of thousands of women . . . after the dragon is *born* at Greenham *she* will be taken by women from another country, to another celebration for life. This is the start of *her* journey around the earth, spreading and joining women's creativity and strength' (my italics). The whole ideology of 'women's creativity' as limited to traditional 'domestic' forms and to birth – both metaphoric and literal – has become reinforced by these so-called feminist activities. Most revealing of all is this description of 'keening' (a sort of high-pitched whine): 'Keening is something traditionally done by women and is now confined to mourning. It's a means of expression without words, without having to get tied up in various arguments, facts and figures, whys and wherefores. You can just show how you feel'.

But is 'just showing how you feel' always the best way to

convince others of your cause? The notion of self-expression has taken on a major role in women's anti-nuclear activities, and while there is clearly a positive value in this for the women concerned, sometimes the means to an end becomes an end in itself. 'Every now and then we'd link arms in a big circle and dance around the top of the silo. We were all ecstatic, overtaken by the brilliant feeling that we'd actually done it!'. The *experience* of the action becomes almost a substitute for the *purpose* of the action:

We leapt up. I can only say we had a sort of celebration. We hugged and kissed each other and felt wonderful. It was extraordinary. We felt as if we'd won a victory in a way – a moral victory. Somehow we found ourselves in this enormous circle. I don't know how many of us there were. There were enough to make a really big circle that took up the whole of the road, right from the base fence across to the other side of the road. We took up the whole of the space, dancing and singing for a while. It was lovely. Then one woman suggested that we should stand in silence to calm ourselves down. So we all stood in this enormous circle, smiling in silence for a few minutes. It seemed quite a long time. It was very restful and calming and we felt very close to each other.

Direct action has been a powerful form of publicity for the anti-nuclear campaign, but it can also be seen as a therapeutic outlet for the feelings of powerlessness which are engendered by the very existence of nuclear weapons. Of course it is crucial for people to feel solidarity and strength or there is no emotional fuel for the movement. But as with all political campaigns, many other feelings and values are channelled into the nuclear issue, so that both the weapons and the actions against them come to function in the realm of the *symbolic:* 'The silos . . . are a focal point of all the negative things that are going on in the world – paranoia, greed, misuse of power, violence, a lack of imagination for alternatives. In my mind I saw them as revolting man-made boils on the earth's surface, full of evil. I wanted to let out all the feelings I have about the threat of nuclear war, the fear and the dread. And I wanted to concentrate on the future, to feel optimistic . . . I kept thinking about celebrating life. What actually happened was that I did that. When we got to the silos, even though we were so excited, I stood quietly for a few minutes, with my eyes closed, and let it all drain out of me.' Many of these descriptions give the impression that symbolic acts are not seen as such, but *feel* to the participants as if they have a direct effect. Dancing on silos does not get rid of them.

But it does attract media and public attention to them. The women at Greenham have forced the media to focus on the nuclear issue and have mobilized public opinion all over the country. It is here that the emphasis on the family, parenthood, and people's individual responsibilities, becomes so effective: turning society's own values against itself, showing how the government's policies undermine and threaten those very institutions and relations it claims to cherish – the family unit and parental control. When Mrs Thatcher announces that parents should take more responsibility for their children, and a mother can reply that she is doing just that by fighting against nuclear weapons, there is a publicity score for the anti-nuclear movement that Saatchi and Saatchi would be glad to have thought up. As one woman says: 'I've got two young children, and I've taken responsibility for their passage into adulthood. Everyone tells me they are my responsibility. The government tells me this. It is my responsibility to create a world fit for them to grow up in. I can't say I'm responsible for my children not catching whooping cough and *not* responsible for doing anything about the threat of annihilation which hangs over them . . .'. Babies with badges, women holding hands in non-violent (and essentially non-effective) protest – all these are the perfect media images to catch the sympathy of any 'feeling person' and to illustrate the essential righteousness of the anti-nuclear cause. Such an important and broad-based campaign has to tap whatever popular sentiments it can, to gain support; and the nuclear family is a highly efficient propaganda weapon. But do we really need to believe our own propaganda? The government constructs its defence of missile policies (c.f. party political broadcasts and 'The Peace Game') in the form of advertisements, complete with persuasive male voice-over selling us the nuclear detergent to protect our homes and children. If we are to meet them on their own ground, let us at least do it with our eyes wide open.

(1984)

THREE KINDS OF DIRT

How many kinds of dirt are there?

This question might seem to belong in the realm of linguistics, along with the Eskimos' eighteen words for 'white', which are often used to show how language arbitrarily divides the continuum of the colour spectrum in ways that vary from culture to culture. Some languages have no word for 'brown', others distinguish several kinds of blue; and these divisions form the grid which patterns experience itself, since it is hard to perceive and describe something you have no words for. In every basic linguistics class the same examples are used, derived from Saussure's *Course in General Linguistics:* the French 'mouton' does not distinguish between dead or alive sheep, while for us, 'mutton' makes the distinction, and hence produces meanings slightly different from those accessible in French. The language of each culture does not so much name the world, as define its possibilities. Lacking the Eskimos' graded scale of whiteness, so appropriate in their snowy surroundings, we find it hard actually to *see* 'white' as anything other than one colour – though Persil advertisers would have it otherwise.

This brings us back to dirt. A scientific answer to the question above is found in the *Hoover Book of Home Management,* under the caption *What is Carpet Dirt?:* 'Day to day soiling can be divided into five groups but the first three are the most important.' These turn out to be, *(1) Surface Litter, (2) Light, Clinging Dust* and *(3) Heavy Dirt and Grit.* Besides lists of their ingredients, we are given warnings of the particular dangers posed by each type of dirt. *Surface Litter* clings recriminatingly to the surface of the pile, making the carpet look uncared for, while although *Light, Clinging Dust* penetrates the pile, some of it always remains on the surface to give a dull, dingy look. In extreme cases it *could* cause carpet rot. *Heavy Dirt and Grit* hold a different kind of menace, for they may lurk undetected: *'a carpet is able to hold its own weight in grit, and yet look fairly normal'.*

In case these varied threats should seem like the figment of someone's imagination, a scientific diagram reveals, through a cross-section of a typical carpet, precisely the *three kinds of dirt.* Beneath this diagram is another, demonstrating, logically enough, the *three cleaning principles* which can banish them.

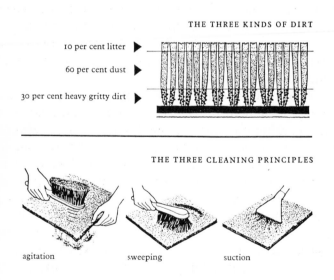

THE THREE KINDS OF DIRT

10 per cent litter ▶

60 per cent dust ▶

30 per cent heavy gritty dirt ▶

THE THREE CLEANING PRINCIPLES

agitation   sweeping   suction

The following section is called *Choosing a Vacuum Cleaner.* 'It is wise to select one which will remove all three kinds of dirt.' You bet, after hearing what those three can do! And of course, this is the *Hoover* book of home management. Each attachment of your Hoover corresponds to some natural function dictated by the very nature of dirt itself! The two *other* types of carpet soiling, which are less important, are, revealingly, those which cannot be treated by vacuuming since they are *(4) Sticky, Greasy Substances* (although there is a Hoover shampooer to deal with this) and finally, *(5) Marks and Stains.*

Generously, the *Hoover Book of Home Management* recommends various other brand names when it comes to aspects of homecare outside its own province. But in every case, the product, whether a cleanser or a kitchen suite, is wheeled on as the 'answer' to a 'problem', while in fact the product itself defines the problem it claims to solve. Carpet dirt is dealt with, only to give way to the problems of the *absorbed stain,* the *built-up stain* and the *compound stain.* Twenty years later, we are more familiar with different categories, such as the *biological* stain and the *'biological' washing powder* which is required to combat it. No matter that the washing powder is in fact a *chemical* substance, it must be named to match the stain. The product must distinguish itself from its rivals.

And it does this by defining the world around it, creating new categories out of previously undifferentiated areas of experience. Different kinds of smell require different kinds of deodorant, *'intimate'* and otherwise. (Can a deodorant *be un*intimate?). A short while ago we had a new kind of stain, the *'under stain'* which now seems to have disappeared. Instead, we have stains which say 'Hot', though the label says Not. (What they are really crying for, in their coded language, is Ariel detergent.) But there are not only different kinds of dirt, there are different kinds of clean: squeaky clean, Persil White, and the peculiar expanding towels and woollens which have to be pressed down into drawers and will hardly lie still after being treated with fabric softener.

If it is language that channels our physical perceptions, it is the language of consumer products which defines our daily life. Whether we feel consciously 'for' or 'against' consumer society, the terms of our experience, the language of our delight or protest, are the same. I may hold out against buying a conditioner as well as a shampoo – but I cannot wish it out of existence, or ignore the fact that it is associated with healthy, shining hair and that this is desirable. The world of consumerism is the one we live in – it is too late to opt out: but there are two important questions – one, what we say in the language available, the other, what that language itself means.

For the meanings and uses of products cannot be entirely controlled; they can be appropriated and turned around on the society which produces them. Fashion is perhaps the area where the products of consumerism are most obviously rearranged to spell rebellion: in a curious paradox, the more fashionable (in street terms, that is) – the more rebellious. Those who are comfortable within society may like to go around looking like that, but there is a kind of sharpness in dress which is an act of aggression against the 'normal'. Of course, the rapid turnover which is such an essential part of fashion is also ideally suited to the profit-making industries which supply the young and stylish. It is hard to separate the two things: in many aspects the 'anti-social' is patterned in the same form as the social.

Products map out the social world, defining, not what we do, but the ways in which we can conceive of doing things – rather as a building maps out space. Not that products are the originators of any ideology, rather they embody possibilities whose boundaries are more revealing than any one possible use. The most telling thing about a product is usually what you *can't* do with it. It is, broadly speaking, the same form of society which two hundred years ago initiated the *cell* system in prisons and asylums, that has today produced the *one-way TV:* a commodity which is limited to individual reception, when TV technology could equally easily be used for two-way and multiple transmission. The limitation on the use of this particular product simply measures the extent to which individualism and passivity are taken for granted in our society generally. This is also built into the form of, for example, the lecture theatre; which makes discussion among the 'audience' almost physically impossible.

Buildings and technology clearly divide up our social space and vision into shapes which are much more permanent than their content. But all products are part of this material landscape, whose contours chart our very vision of life and its possibilities, and whose boundaries mark out our channels of thought. These are not fixed, but they cannot be shifted by an opposition which fits the same slots. Every society has some kind of map, a grid of the terms available to think in at any given time. In ours, consumer goods are just some of the chief landmarks which define the 'natural' categories we are accustomed to. It takes the law to define 'crime'; it takes medicine to define 'sickness'; it takes science to define 'nature'; and it takes *Hoover* to define the *three kinds of dirt.*

(1984)

THE POLITICS OF CONSUMPTION

Ever since Richard Hoggart's attempt to grapple with the 'consumerization' of the working class in *The Uses of Literacy,* the politics of consumption have been on the agenda for the left in some form or another. In recent years, particularly within the field of cultural studies, there has been a growing interest in consumerism not as regressive (a position put in much of Jeremy Seabrook's writing) but as a progressive trend – for example in studies of fashion and subcultural activities where commodities or styles can be 'subverted' into rebellious statements. The extreme form of this is found in the academic idea of 'postmodernism' where, because no meanings are fixed and anything can be used to mean anything else, one can claim as radical almost anything provided it is taken out of its original context.

The original context of any product is that of its production. The one feature shared by both Hoggart, whose argument is limited to the sphere of leisure and domestic culture, and the cultural studies post-punk stylists, whose concern is with the meanings of consumerism alone, is an absence of any sense of a relationship between the spheres of production and consumption. Because if the product's context is, first of all, its production, what is the context of the consumer, without whom, after all, there can be no consumption? It is the context of a society in which the majority of people have no control whatsoever over their productive lives: no security, little choice in work if they have work at all, and no means of public expression. In this society, consuming is, for those who can afford it, a major form of cultural and social activity and at the same time a central feature of the economy which is imposing such frustrations in the first place. The production of an ever-increasing range of consumer goods is crucial to modern capitalism while the consumption of those goods is crucial not only to the economy but to the ideology which supports it. Marx chose to begin his great study of the capitalist system with – the commodity; not because of its economic role alone, but because of what it *means*.

The conscious, chosen meaning in most people's lives comes much more from what they consume than what they produce. Clothes, interiors, furniture, records, knick-knacks, all the things that we buy involve decisions and the exercise of our own judgement, choice, 'taste'. Obviously we don't choose what is available for us to choose between in the first place. Consuming seems to offer a certain scope for creativity, rather like a toy where all the parts are pre-chosen but the combinations are multiple. Consumerism is often represented as a supremely individualistic act – yet it is also very social: shopping is a socially endorsed event, a form of social cement. It makes you feel normal. Most people find it cheers them up – even window shopping. The extent to which shoplifting is done where there is no material need (most items stolen are incredibly trivial) reveals the extent to which people's wants and needs are *translated* into the form of consumption.

Buying and owning, in our society, offer a sense of control. If you pay for something you do tend to feel you control it; a belief borne out by people's eagerness to buy British Telecom shares regardless of the fact that they *already* owned BT. Yet the idea of having a stake in society

or a tiny voting right in a public institution is not of itself
reactionary, only the form it appears in. Although at present
the left shies away from many issues of public ownership,
surely the enormous rush of small-scale BT investors shows,
not that everyone is a rabid 'Thatcherite', but that a great
many 'ordinary' people do want 'a stake in this country' –
something which they (like so many NHS patients) were
evidently not made to *feel* they had when it was owned by
the state.

Ownership is at present the *only* form of control legitimized in our culture. Any serious attempts at controlling
products from the other side – as with the miners' demand to
control the future of *their* product, coal (or the printing
unions' attempts to control their product, newspaper articles, etc) are not endorsed. Some parts of the left find these
struggles less riveting than the struggles over meanings in
street style. Yet underlying *both* struggles is the need for
people to control their environment and produce their own
communal identity; it is just that the former, if won, could
actually fulfil that need while the latter ultimately never will.
'Progressive' socialists who argue that 'Thatcherism' has
captured many popular needs are quite right – but while
such needs are *captured* by this system they are precisely *not*
fulfilled by it, in the way that they could be by a more daring
socialism.

The point about consumerism is that people are getting
something out of it – but something which the left must be
able to offer *in a different form*. The current drift towards
right-wing programmes on the left – e.g. the sale of council
houses – because they are 'popular', ignores the possibility
that many needs and ideals currently fulfilled by – to pursue
this example – the ideology of home ownership, could be
met in different ways. Some of the left seems now to have
accepted the bourgeois equation of private ownership with
freedom and the devolution of power – precisely the
concepts behind Mrs Thatcher's election victories. It is as if

the left can think of no other way to win than by imitating its enemies. The reason council tenants want to buy their houses is quite simple. They are not besotted with the idea of *ownership;* they are gripped by the need for *security.* The key emotions underpinning the dream of home ownership for most council tenants are the desires for control, autonomy and continuity. It should be possible for *public* housing to provide these by, for example, building into its principles the notion of the control of the individual tenant and in practice giving Council tenants the feeling that their Council flat or house *is* 'their' home.

The analysis of consumer items as the concrete forms taken by particular needs is essential if socialists are to envisage different ways of meeting them. As many have pointed out, street fashion is often an attempt to subvert, create, provoke. The TV and video boom shows not only a trend towards the privatization of entertainment but offers the ability to *control,* say, a film on video in the same way one can control when and how one reads a book. The phenomenon of the Walkman provides both a symbolic and a physical means of cutting off from a society which itself appears deaf to, in particular, the young people who form a large proportion of the walkman market. In analyzing these products we can understand more about the society which both produces and uses them. But their forms are fundamentally those of a market capitalism – which they reflect, rather than shape. What *are* potentially radical are the needs that underlie their use: needs both sharpened and denied by the economic system that makes them.

In this sense the economic and the ideological need not be seen – and are not experienced – as separate. Economic oppression is a large part of the powerlessness which consumer ideology seeks to overcome, or, for the very many whose only consumption is barely at the level of necessity, to confirm. The possession of expensive jogging shoes, videos, home computers and so on does not necessarily mark a level of fulfilment for the supposedly right-wing 'bourgeoisified' working class but, in part at least, a measure of frustration. Their aspirations have been caught up in the wheel of consumer production. Wearing a Lacoste sweatshirt doesn't make anyone middle class any more than wearing legwarmers makes you a feminist. The idea that ideologies – including consumer fads – are increasingly 'cut loose' from the economic 'base' has become more and more fashionable on the academic left at a time when these levels have perhaps rarely been more obviously connected. But there are several specific reasons for this view. One is quite simply that a rather demoralized generation of the '60s left, who once looked on discos and TV as the opium of the masses, have recently 'discovered' style – i.e. that you too can dye your hair red, read *The Face* and no longer feel guilty about all those ideologically unsound records and all that Habitat furniture. While nothing is especially wrong with these things, the trend towards seeing consuming as a 'semi-autonomous' ideological phenomenon is definitely, for those left theorists concerned, a bit of a relief. Of course, the great irony is that it is precisely the *illusion* of autonomy which makes consumerism such an effective diversion from the lack of other kinds of power in people's lives. At a time when such power in the political and economic spheres seems very distant, the realm of the 'superstructure' is, for consumers and Marxists alike, a much more fun place to be. Certainly it offers more fun than trying to deal with the frustrations channelled into it but created, predominantly, by the economic realities which are still the major constriction on most people's lives. And also more fun than trying to envisage *new* ways in which some of the needs and desires appropriated by consumer goods can be met.

(*New Socialist*, 1985)

SELECT BIBLIOGRAPHY

This bibliography lists all books, essays and articles (other than newspaper articles) which are quoted, referred to or drawn on directly in the text. It is not a comprehensive further reading list on the subjects covered.

ALTHUSSER, Louis, 'Ideology and Ideological State Apparatuses' in *Lenin and Philosophy and Other Essays*. London: New Left Books, 1971. New York: Monthly Review Press, 1972.

BACHELARD, Gaston, *The Poetics of Space*. Boston: Beacon Press, 1969.

BARENTS, Els, (Introduction) *Cindy Sherman Catalogue*. Munich: Schirmer/Mosel, 1982.

BARTHES, Roland, *Mythologies*. New York: Hill and Wang, 1972. London: Paladin, 1973
Image-Music-Text. London: Fontana, 1977. New York: Hill & Wang, 1978.

BAUDRY, Jean-Louis, 'Writing, Fiction, Ideology', *Afterimage* (UK) No. 5, Spring 1974.

BEER, Olivier, *Pas de Deux*. London: Pavanne, 1982.

BENJAMIN, Walter, 'A Short History of Photography' (first published 1931) *Screen* Vol. 13 No. 1, Spring 1972.
'The Work of Art in the Age of Mechanical Reproduction' in *Illuminations*. New York: Schocken Books, 1969. London: Fontana, 1970.
'The Author as Producer' in *Understanding Brecht*. London: New Left Books, 1973.

BOURDIEU, Pierre, 'The Aristocracy of Culture' and 'The Production of Belief: Contribution to an Economy of Symbolic Goods' in *Media, Culture and Society* 1980, No. 2.

BRECHT, Bertolt, *The Messingkauf Dialogues*. London: Eyre Methuen, 1965.
Poems Parts 1, 2 & 3. London: Eyre Methuen, 1976.

BROWN, Helen Gurley, *Sex and the Single Girl*. New York: Avon Books, 1983. London: Four Square Books, 1963.
Having It All. New York: Simon & Schuster, 1982. London: Sidgwick & Jackson, 1983.

CLARK, Jane, and SIMMONDS, Diana, *Move Over Misconceptions*, British Film Institute Dossier No. 4 (Doris Day). London 1980.

COOK, Alice and KIRK, Gwyn, *Greenham Women Everywhere*. London: Pluto Press, 1983.

EISENSTEIN, Serge, *The Film Sense*. London: Faber, 1943. New York: Harvest Books, 1969.

ENGELS, Frederick, *The Origin of the Family, Private Property and the State* in *Selected Works*. London: Lawrence and Wishart, 1958. New York: International Pubs., 1972.

ENZENSBERGER, Hans Magnus, 'Constituents of a Theory of the Media' in *Raids and Reconstructions*. London: Pluto Press, 1976.

FOUCAULT, Michel, *The Order of Things*. London: Tavistock, 1970. New York: Random House, 1973.
The History of Sexuality: Volume 1: An Introduction. London: Allen Lane, 1979. New York: Vintage Books, 1980.

FREEMAN, Gillian, *An Easter Egg Hunt*. London: Pavanne, 1982.

FREUD, Sigmund, *Three Essays on Sexuality*. London: Hogarth Press, 1953. New York: Basic Books, 1982.
The Interpretation of Dreams. London: Hogarth Press, 1953. New York: Avon Books, 1971.
The Psychopathology of Everyday Life. London: Hogarth Press, 1960. New York: Norton, 1971.

GRAMSCI, Antonio, *Selections from the Prison Notebooks*. London: London: Lawrence & Wishart, 1971. New York: International Pubs, 1971.

HALE, Chris, 'Punishment and the Visible' in *The Prison Film*. Radical Alternatives to Prison, London 1982.

HALL, Stuart, 'The Great Moving Right Show', *Marxism Today*, January 1979.

HARVEY, Jane, *The Hoover Book of Home Management*. London: Hutchinson, 1963.

HARVEY, Sylvia, 'Woman's Place: The Absent Family of Film Noir' in *Women in Film Noir* (ed. E. Ann Kaplan), British Film Institute, London 1980. US: University of Illinois Press, 1980.

HASKELL, Molly, *From Reverence to Rape: The Treatment of Women in the Movies*. New York: Holt, Rinehart & Winston, 1974. London: New English Library, 1975.

HEBDIGE, Dick, *Subculture: The Meaning of Style*. London/New York: Methuen, 1979.

HIRSCH, Julia, *Family Photographs*. New York/London: Oxford University Press, 1981.

HOGGART, Richard, *The Uses of Literacy*. London: Chatto & Windus 1957.

KENNEDY, Raymond, *Columbine*. London: Pavanne, 1982.

KUPFERMANN, Jeannette, *The MsTaken Body*. London: Granada (Paladin), 1981.

LADAS, Alice, WHIPPLE, Beverley and PERRY, Rev. John, *The G Spot and Other Recent Discoveries about Human Sexuality*. New York: Holt, Rinehart & Winston, 1982. London: Corgi Books, 1983.

LE DOEUFF, Michele, 'Women and Philosophy', *Radical Philosophy* No. 17, summer 1977.

MARX, Karl, *Capital Volume 1*, London: Lawrence & Wishart, 1970. New York: International Pubs., 1967.
Economic and Philosophical Manuscripts in *Early Writings*. London: Pelican, 1975. New York: McGraw-Hill, 1963.

MARX, Karl and ENGELS, Frederick, *The German Ideology*. London: Lawrence & Wishart, 1970. New York: International Pubs., 1970.

MISS PIGGY, *Miss Piggy's Guide to Life*. New York: Knopf, 1981, London: Muppet Press/Michael Joseph, 1981.

MITCHELL, Juliet, *Psychoanalysis and Feminism*. London: Pelican, 1975. New York: Vintage Books, 1975.

MULVEY, Laura, 'Visual Pleasure and Narrative Cinema', *Screen*, Vol. 16 No. 3, Autumn 1975.

MULVEY, Laura and WOLLEN, Peter, Script of 'Riddles of the Sphinx', *Screen* Vol. 18 No. 2, Summer 1977.

NIETZSCHE, Friedrich, *Beyond Good and Evil*. London/New York: Penguin, 1973.

ORBACH, Susie, *Fat is a Feminist Issue*. London: Hamlyn, 1979. New York: Berkley Publishing Co., 1982.

PIERCE, C. S., *Collected Papers*. US: Harvard University Press, Cambridge, 1931–58.

ROWBOTHAM, Sheila, *Woman's Consciousness, Man's World.* London/New York: Penguin, 1973.

SAUSSURE, Ferdinand de, Course in General Linguistics. New York: McGraw-Hill, 1966.

SEABROOK, Jeremy, *What Went Wrong?* London: Gollancz, 1978.

STARENKO, Michael, 'What's an Artist To Do? A Short History of Postmodernism and Photography', *Afterimage* (US) January 1983.

STONE, Lawrence, *The Family, Sex and Marriage in England 1500–1800.* London: Pelican, 1979. New York: Harper Row, 1980.

STREET, Pamela, *Light of Evening.* London: Pavanne, 1982.

TROTSKY, Leon, *Literature and Revolution.* Ann Arbor: University of Michigan Press, 1960.

WOLLEN, Peter, *Signs and Meaning in the Cinema.* London: Secker & Warburg, 1969. US: Indiana University Press, 1973.

ZARETSKY, Eli, *Capitalism, the Family and Personal Life.* New York: Harper Row, 1976. London: Pluto Press, 1976.

ACKNOWLEDGEMENTS

The author wishes to thank all the companies for permission to reproduce the advertisements and illustrations published in this volume, and in particular gratefully acknowledges the assistance of Miss M. Corbridge of the National Dairy Council who supplied the picture on p. 216.

Photograph of Falklands Victory Parade by Barry Lewis/ Network, photographs by Cindy Sherman courtesy of Metro Pictures, New York, film stills courtesy of Artificial Eye Film Company, Warner Bros, 20th Century-Fox and the Stills Library of the National Film Archive, London.

Lyrics to 'Modern Girl' by Dominic Bugatti and Frank Musker © 1979 Pendulum Music/Sea Shanty/Chappell Music Ltd, reproduced by kind permission of Chappell Music Ltd.
Lyrics to 'Picture This' by D. Harry, C. Stein and J. Destri © Chrysalis Music Ltd, reproduced by kind permission of Chrysalis Music Ltd.
Lyrics to 'Hollywood Nights' by Bob Seger © 1978 Gear Publishing Co, reproduced by kind permission of Gear Publishing Co.